The Ultimate AHAA Guide

ISBN 978-1-912557-87-5

Published by *RAR Medical Services Limited*
www.uniadmissions.co.uk
info@uniadmissions.co.uk
Tel: +44 (0) 208 068 0438

This book is neither created nor endorsed by Cambridge Assessment. The authors and publisher are not affiliated with Cambridge Assessment. The information offered in this book is purely advisory and any advice given should be taken within this context. As such, the publishers and authors accept no liability whatsoever for the outcome of any applicant's AHAA performance, the outcome of any university applications or for any other loss. Although every precaution has been taken in the preparation of this book, the publisher and author assume no responsibility for errors or omissions of any kind. Neither is any liability assumed for damages resulting from the use of information contained herein. This does not affect your statutory rights.

This book contains passages which deal with racism, sexism, and gender issues, among other controversial topics.

About the Author

Matthew is the **Head of Books** at *UniAdmissions* and is responsible for all published resources. He graduated from King's College, London and Emmanuel College, Cambridge. Over the last five years, he has tutored dozens of successful Oxbridge applicants in the UK, Europe, and China. He has also worked for Oliver Wyman, and Unilever, written for the New Statesman and the Independent, as well as teaching both postgraduates and undergraduates at the Guangxi University for Nationalities in Nanning, China.

Rohan is the **Director of Operations** at *UniAdmissions* and is responsible for its technical and commercial arms. He graduated from Gonville and Caius College, Cambridge and is a fully qualified doctor. Over the last five years, he has tutored hundreds of successful Oxbridge and Medical applicants. He has also authored twenty books on admissions tests and interviews.

Rohan has taught physiology to undergraduates and interviewed medical school applicants for Cambridge. He has published research on bone physiology and writes education articles for the Independent and Huffington Post. In his spare time, Rohan enjoys playing the piano and table tennis.

The Ultimate AHAA Guide

600 Practice Questions

Matthew W Elliott

Rohan Agarwal

UniAdmissions

The Basics

What is the AHAA?

The Arts & Humanities Admissions Assessment (AHAA) is a 2 hour written exam for prospective Cambridge applicants for.

What does the AHAA consist of?

Section	Timing	FORMAT	Questions
ONE	60 Minutes	1A: Thinking Skills	36 Multiple Choice Questions
TWO	60 Minutes	Essay Task	One Essay

Why is the AHAA used?

Cambridge applicants tend to be a bright bunch and therefore usually have excellent grades. The vast majority of applicants score greater than 90% in all of their A level subjects, making it difficult to differentiate between them. This means that competition is fierce, so Cambridge uses the AHAA to help differentiate between applicants.

When do I sit AHAA?

The AHAA takes place in the first week of November every year.

Can I resit the AHAA?

No, you can only sit the AHAA once per admissions cycle.

Where do I sit the AHAA?

You can usually sit the AHAA at your school or college (ask your exams officer for more information). Alternatively, if your school isn't a registered test centre or you're not attending a school or college, you can sit the AHAA at an authorised test centre.

Do I have to resit the AHAA if I reapply?

If you reapply, you will have to resit the AHAA. This ensures that all applicants are being compared in a fair and equitable manner.

How is the AHAA Scored?

In section 1, each question carries one mark and there is no negative marking. In section 2, your answer will be assessed based on the argument and also its clarity.

How is the AHAA used?

Different Cambridge colleges will place different weightings on different components so it's important you find out as much information about how your marks will be used by emailing the college admissions office.

In general, the university will interview a high proportion of realistic applicants so the AHAA score isn't vital for making the interview shortlist. However, it can play a huge role in the final decision after your interview.

Getting a great score on the AHAA won't guarantee you a place or an interview, but your chances of being interviewed if you score in bottom few percentiles are slim.

General Advice

Start Early

It is much easier to prepare if you practice little and often. Start your preparation well in advance; ideally by mid September but at the latest by early October. This way you will have plenty of time to complete all five available papers and won't have to panic and cram just before the test, which is a much less effective and more stressful way to learn. In general, an early start will give you the opportunity to identify the complex issues and work at your own pace.

Prioritise

Some questions in section 1 can be complex – and given the intense time pressure you need to know your limits. It is essential that you don't get stuck with very difficult questions. If a question looks particularly long or complex, mark it for review and move on. You don't want to be caught 5 questions short at the end just because you took more than 3 minutes in answering a challenging question. If a question is taking too long, choose a sensible answer and move on. Remember that each question carries equal weighting and therefore, you should adjust your timing in accordingly. With practice and discipline, you can get very good at this and learn to maximise your efficiency.

Positive Marking

There are no penalties for incorrect answers in the AHAA; you will gain one for each right answer and will not get one for each wrong or unanswered one. This provides you with the luxury that you can always guess should you absolutely be not able to figure out the right answer for a question or run behind time. Since each question provides you with 4 possible answers, you have a 25% chance of guessing correctly. Therefore, if you aren't sure (and are running short of time), then make an educated guess and move on. Before 'guessing' you should try to eliminate a couple of answers to increase your chances of getting the question correct. For example, if a question has 4 options and you manage to eliminate 2 options- your chances of getting the question increase from 25% to 50%!

Avoid losing easy marks on other questions because of poor exam technique. If you were to guess the answer to every question in Section 1, you would expect to score 25%, so make sure to provide an answer to every question, even if you only have a few minutes left at the end of the exam.

Practice

This is the best way of familiarising yourself with the style of questions and the timing for this section. You are unlikely to be familiar with the style of questions when you first encounter them. Therefore, you want to be comfortable at using this before you sit the test.

Practising questions will put you at ease and make you more comfortable with the exam. The more comfortable you are, the less you will panic on the test day and the more likely you are to score highly. Initially, work through the questions at your own pace, and spend time carefully reading the questions and looking at any additional data. When it becomes closer to the test, **make sure you practice the questions under exam conditions**.

Past Papers

The AHAA is a relatively new exam so there is only limited specimen papers available. The specimen papers are freely available online at **www.uniadmissions.co.uk/AHAA**. You can find worked solutions to the specimen paper at the end of this book, and we recommend you attempt it after completing the four Practice Papers in this book.

A word on timing...

You have 60 minutes to complete section one which means that you will have 100 seconds per question; this may sound like a lot but given that you're often required to read and analyse long passages - it can often not be enough. Some questions in this section are very tricky and can be a big drain on your limited time. **The people who fail to complete section 1 are those who get bogged down on a particular question**.

Therefore, it is vital that you start to get a feel for which questions are going to be easy and quick to do and which ones should be left till the end. The best way to do this is through practice and the questions in this book will offer extensive opportunities for you to do so.

"If you had all day to do your AHAA, you would get 100%. But you don't."

While this isn't completely true, it illustrates a very important point. Once you've practiced and know how to answer the questions, the clock is your biggest enemy. This seemingly obvious statement has one very important consequence. **The way to improve your AHAA score is to improve your speed.** There is no magic bullet. But there are a great number of techniques that, with practice, will give you significant time gains, allowing you to answer more questions and score more marks.

Timing is tight throughout the AHAA – **mastering timing is the first key to success**. Some candidates choose to work as quickly as possible to save up time at the end to check back, but this is generally not the best way to do it. AHAA questions can have a lot of information in them – each time you start answering a question it takes time to get familiar with the instructions and information. By splitting the question into two sessions (the first run-through and the return-to-check) you double the amount of time you spend on familiarising yourself with the data, as you have to do it twice instead of only once. This costs valuable time. In addition, candidates who do check back may spend 2–3 minutes doing so and yet not make any actual changes. Whilst this can be reassuring, it is a false reassurance as it is unlikely to have a significant effect on your actual score. Therefore, it is usually best to pace yourself very steadily, aiming to spend the same amount of time on each question and finish the final question in a section just as time runs out. This reduces the time spent on re-familiarising with questions and maximises the time spent on the first attempt, gaining more marks.

It is essential that you don't get stuck with the hardest questions – no doubt there will be some. In the time spent answering only one of these you may miss out on answering three easier questions. If a question is taking too long, choose a sensible answer and move on. Never see this as giving up or in any way failing, rather it is the smart way to approach a test with a tight time limit. With practice and discipline, you can get very good at this and learn to maximise your efficiency. It is not about being a hero and aiming for full marks – this is almost impossible and unnecessary. It is about maximising your efficiency and gaining the maximum possible number of marks within the time you have.

Top tip! Ensure that you take a watch that can show you the time in seconds into the exam. This will allow you have a much more accurate idea of the time you're spending on a question. In general, if you've spent more than 2 minutes on a question – move on regardless of how close you think you are to finishing it.

Section 1

This is the first section of the AHAA and as you walk in, it is inevitable that you will feel nervous. Make sure that you have been to the toilet because once it starts you cannot simply pause and go. Take a few deep breaths and calm yourself down. Remember that panicking will not help and may negatively affect your marks- so try and avoid this as much as possible.

Because the AHAA is a new exam, it can feel difficult to prepare, as your teachers and tutors will have very limited experience of it. However, there are still powerful shortcuts and techniques that you can use to improve your performance.

Section 1 is the multiple choice section. In the exam, you will be presented with four sets of passages of varying lengths and be asked between 2-12 questions per passage. There is a total of 60 minutes for this section and you cannot use any of the time for Section 2 in Section 1 – you only have a maximum of 60 minutes.

The aim of this section is to test your comprehension, interpretation and deduction skills, while working with the kind of materials you would work with while studying at Cambridge.

This tests your ability to understand the different parts of a passage. It is important to understand what constitutes a good argument:
1. **Evidence:** Arguments which are heavily based on value judgements and subjective statements tend to be weaker than those based on facts, statistics and the available evidence.
2. **Logic**: A good argument should flow and the constituent parts should fit well into an overriding view or belief.
3. **Balance:** A good argument must concede that there are other views or beliefs (counter-argument). The key is to carefully dismantle these ideas and explain why they are wrong.

Sometimes, the question requires you to consider whether an argument is 'strong' or 'weak'. All arguments include reasons (premises) which aim to support a conclusion. Here, we are considering whether the reasons provide weak or strong support.

The parts of an argument:
An argument is an untimely attempt to persuade with the use of reasons. This can be distinguished from an assertion, which is simply a statement of fact or belief.

Assertion: It is raining outside.
Argument: I can hear the continuous sound of water splashing on the roof. Therefore, it must be raining outside.

The argument involves an attempt to persuade another that it is raining and it includes a reason as to why the speaker thinks it is raining, which is the splashing on the roof. The assertion, on the other hand, is not backed up with a reason – it is simply a statement.

An argument involves a premise and a conclusion.
A premise is simply a statement from which another can be inferred or follows as a conclusion.
A conclusion though is a summary of the arguments made.

For example:
>   **Premise 1:** All dogs bark.
>   **Premise 2:** My pet is a dog.
>   **Conclusion:** My pet barks.

The conclusion here follows from both of the premises.

Explanation

Sometimes, it will be necessary to distinguish an argument from an explanation and you will need to be careful here as it can be difficult to distinguish sometimes. In essence, an argument will always involve an attempt to persuade the reader as to a point of view. Explanations, on the other hand, do not. Explanations may describe why something is the way it is or account for how something has occurred.

For example:

1. **Explanation:** We can hear the sound of water drops because the tap is leaking.
2. **Argument:** We can hear the sound of water drops. Therefore, we need to call the plumber.

Example 1 just accounts for *why* water drops can be heard – there is no attempt to persuade the reader that there are either water drops or that the tap is leaking. The tap leaking is just asserted as an explanation for the sound of the water drops.

In example 2, the author is advancing an argument as the author is making the case to call the plumber. The premise being the sound of water drops.

Premise vs. Conclusion

- A **Conclusion** is a summary of the arguments being made and is usually explicitly stated or heavily implied.
- A **Premise** is a statement from which another statement can be inferred or follows as a conclusion.

Hence, a conclusion is shown/implied/proven by a premise. Similarly, a premise shows/indicates/establishes a conclusion. Consider for example: *My mum, being a woman, is clever as all women are clever.*

Premise 1: My mum is a woman + **Premise 2:** Women are clever = **Conclusion:** My mum is clever.

This is fairly straightforward as it's a very short passage and the conclusion is explicitly stated. Sometimes the latter may not happen. Consider: *My mum is a woman and all women are clever.*

Here, whilst the conclusion is not explicitly being stated, both premises still stand and can be used to reach the same conclusion.

You may sometimes be asked to identify if any of the options cannot be "reliably concluded". This is effectively asking you to identify why an option **cannot** be the conclusion. There are many reasons why but the most common ones are:

1. Over-generalising: *My mum is clever therefore all women are clever.*
2. Being too specific: *All kids like candy thus my son also likes candy.*
3. Confusing Correlation vs. Causation: *Lung cancer is much more likely in patients who drink water. Hence, water causes lung cancer.*
4. Confusing Cause and Effect: *Lung cancer patients tend to smoke so it follows that having lung cancer must make people want to smoke.*

Note how conjunctives like hence, thus, therefore, and it follows, give you a clue as to when a conclusion is being stated. More examples of these include: "it follows that, implies that, whence, entails that".

Similarly, words like "because, as indicated by, in that, given that, due to the fact that" usually identify premises.

Assumptions

It is important to be able to identify assumptions in a passage as questions frequently ask to identify these.

An assumption is a reasonable assertion that can be made based on the available evidence.

A crucial difference between an assumption and a premise is that a premise is normally mentioned in the passage, whereas an assumption is not. A useful way to consider whether there is a particular assumption in the passage is to consider whether the conclusion relies on it to work – i.e. if the assumption is taken away, does that affect the conclusion? If it does, then it's an assumption.

> *Top tip!* Don't get confused between premises and assumptions. A **premise** is a statement that is explicitly stated in the passage. An **assumption** is an inference that is made from the passage.

Fact vs. Opinion

Sometimes you will be required to distinguish between a fact and an opinion. A fact is something that can be tested to be true or false. An opinion, on the other hand, cannot be tested to be true or false – it is someone's view on something and is a value judgement.

For example: "Tuition fees were reduced by the Welsh government in 2012. Many viewed this as a fair outcome."

Fact: Tuition fees were reduced by the Welsh government.
Opinion: It is a fair outcome.
> What one person sees as being 'fair' may not be 'fair' to another person – even if many people see a particular policy as fair. It is a normative statement that cannot be tested as true or false.

Correlation vs. Causation

Just because two incidents or events have occurred does not mean that one has caused the other. For example: "French people are known for having a glass of wine with dinner and they have a larger life expectancy than we do. Therefore, we should consume wine to be healthier."

This argument is flawed. There are 2 events: (i) French people known for having wine and (ii) French people having a larger life expectancy. There is no suggestion in the extract that (i) wine is causally related to (ii) or that having wine actually leads to a longer life. Accordingly, in itself, the premises do not adequately support the conclusion – there could be other reasons such as diet or exercise.

Approaching Section 1

The Passage

Take every fact in each passage as true and your answer must be based on the information in the passage only – so do not use your own knowledge, even if you feel that you personally know the topic. For example, if the question asks who the first person was to walk on the moon, then states "the three crew members of the first lunar mission were Edwin Aldrin, Neil Armstrong, and Michael Collins". The correct answer is "cannot tell" – even though you know it was Neil Armstrong and see his name, the passage itself does not tell you who left the landing craft first. Likewise, if there is a quotation or an extract from a book which is factually inaccurate, you should answer based on the information available to you rather than what you know to be true.

Read the Questions First

Different strategies work well for different people but indeed, having a look at the questions before going through the passage can help you focus on the important details in the passage in the first reading of it, thereby saving you time. It's best to try this strategy with some of the passages in this book to see if it works for you.

Timing

Even if you finish the questions before 60 minutes run out, you **cannot** use any of this extra time on Section 2 – you can only use this 60 minutes on Section 1 so you might as well go back through any questions that you found difficult or whether you were uncertain in any areas.

Common Types of Questions

➢ What unstated assumption is being made?
➢ Which of the following is an assertion?
➢ What is the main idea in the passage?
➢ What is the main argument in the passage?
➢ Which of the following is an argument in favour of…?
➢ What is meant by?
➢ What conclusion is reached by the author?
➢ Which of the following weakens or strengthens the writer's argument?
➢ Which of the following is an assertion of fact?

Reading Non-Fiction

As well as critically analysing the passages in the book, a brilliant preparation for the AHAA is to engage in further non-fiction reading and to consider some of the following questions:
➢ What issues are being raised?
➢ What assumptions are made?
➢ What is the conclusion?
➢ Is there adequate support for the conclusion?
➢ Whose perspective is it coming from?
➢ How would you create a counter-argument?

Critically reading non-fiction, such as in a quality newspaper, will not only help improve your Section 1 performance but would also improve your knowledge bank for the Section 2 essay.

Top tip! Though it might sound counter-intuitive, it's best to read the question *before* reading the passage. Then you'll have a much better idea of what you're looking for and are therefore more likely to find it quicker.

Practice Paper A

Task One

Read the two abstracts below, which summarise two academic articles on automation.

Abstract One

It has been argued that automation will soon replace most of the work that lawyers currently perform. We point out three main weaknesses with the current literature on automation: (1) a failure to appreciate the limits of existing and emerging software, and a lack of technical detail in general; (2) a lack of data about which tasks lawyers spend the most time on given that only some tasks are capable of being automated; and (3) a lack of consideration about whether algorithmic task performance adequately adheres to the values and aims of the legal profession.

We analyse a data set concerned with how lawyers in large firms spend their time, and we estimate that automation has a far less significant impact on the demand for lawyer's time than is commonly suggested. The existing literature focuses too narrowly on the effects that automation has on legal employment. Instead, it should focus on the myriad of ways in which computers are *changing*, not replacing, the work that lawyers do. Any inquiry into legal automation must start by discussing how computers perform legal tasks differently than humans. Once we know these differences, we will have some idea about whether it is even desirable to automate legal tasks. We may also gain an insight into the core values and goals of the legal profession itself.

Abstract Two

"The book authors argue that professional roles will be entirely supplanted by automated systems. Their theory rests on neoliberal and techno-utopian assumptions which conceal an underlying error: that the role of a professional can be reduced into nothing more than the transmission of expert knowledge. These theorists fail to tackle two central issues about professionalism. Firstly, professionals are often self-employed or self-directed. They work with and for patients, for instance, and not for the benefit of shareholders or CEOS. Secondly, professional freedom is necessary: professionals often navigate complex clashes of values and ethical dilemmas which require discretion, compromise, and personal responsibility. These considerations are fatal the authors' case for full automation of the professions."

Question 1

What do the authors of Abstract One claim about the existing literature?

A) The literature is too detailed in its approach.

B) The literature is too focused on data analysis

C) The literature devotes too much attention to algorithms

D) The opposite of all the above.

Question 2

In Abstract One 'narrow employment effects' are contrasted with what?

A) The transformational impact of computer technologies

B) An emphasis on employee welfare

C) The technical qualifications held by lawyers

D) The complexity of legal language

Question 3

What opinion of the book being reviewed does the author of Abstract Two hold?

A) The book's authors are too Marxist in their analysis

B) The book's authors focus too much on identity.

C) The book's authors argument is fatally flawed

D) The book's style is too dense

Question 4

What critique would the author of Abstract Two be most likely to offer of Abstract One?

A) The analysis is too political in its outlook

B) The analysis is insufficiently data driven

C) The analysis worries too much about the welfare of workers

D) The analysis is too technocratic and techno-utopian

Question 5

According to the authors of abstract 2, what is the underlying error of the book they review?

A) The theory rests on neoliberalism.

B) The authors argue that professional roles will be overtaken by automation.

C) The authors have too reductive a view about professional roles.

D) The authors ignore that professionals are often self-employed.

Question 6

Which abstract or abstracts is critical of the concept of automation?

A) Neither abstract

B) Both abstracts

C) Abstract one only

D) Abstract two only

Task Two

Read the four texts below, which give the views of four writers on gender identity

A) Alex Sharpe
There will be no impact on existing rights of service providers to exclude trans women from female-only spaces if reforms are passed which make it easier for trans people to gain legal recognition of their gender identity. The Equality Act protects people who have the characteristic of 'gender reassignment' from discrimination. However, it also allows for sex-based exceptions that permit discrimination in the context of female-only spaces when this is a proportionate means to achieve a legitimate goal. The government has repeatedly affirmed that it will not alter these provisions.

Those who oppose reform of the Gender Recognition Act claim that trans women who hold a gender recognition certificate will not be subject to the sex-based exceptions because they are, by virtue of the Gender Recognition Act, legally female. Thus, they argue that the Gender Recognition act will virtually eliminate occasions where the sex-based exceptions might be invoked because many more people will be able to acquire a gender recognition certificate.

B) Rosa Freedman
In English law, sex and gender are separate categories. Sex is a legally protected characteristic, but gender identity is not. Trans advocates often use the terms 'sex' and 'gender' interchangeably. However, only by maintaining 'sex' and 'gender' as distinct categories will we be able to address the concerns of transgender people and women as protected, and defined, by the Equality Act.

The benefits of enabling individuals to self-identify as a different gender is that it would remove the long, pathologizing process of obtaining a gender recognition certificate. We propose that in order to self-identify a person must legally declare whether they identify as male, female, or non-binary. They would be issued a certificate which explains why their gender identify differs from their birth certificate sex. This process would be akin to naturalisation.

This should address the concerns of transgender people, including the growing number of people who do not want to identify as either male or female, by creating a neutral 'gender X' as has been done in other countries like the Netherlands.

C) Maureen O'Hara
Allowing people to change their gender identity legally by self-declaration would create major safeguarding concerns for children, vulnerable adults, and women. This is not because transgender individuals are a safeguarding threat in and of themselves. It is because empirical evidence shows that the vast majority of sex offenders are male, and that repeat sex offenders are cunning manipulators who will stop at nothing to gain access to vulnerable people. Self-identification laws would enable these sex offenders to identify as women in order to bypass the Equality Act and access female-only spaces or take up female-only safeguarding roles.

In the parliamentary inquiry into transgender equality, the British Association of Gender Identity specialists and the British Psychological Society both stated that male sex offenders would claim to identify as women in order to more easily commit sexual offences. The British Psychological Society cautioned that we should be "extremely cautious of setting law and policy such that some of the most dangerous people in society have greater latitude".

D) Peter Dunne
Transgender children are currently excluded from the Gender Recognition Act. The Act states that only people aged 18 or over can apply for a gender recognition certificate. The government has not proposed to enlarge legal recognition to transgender youth.

The exclusion of transgender minors from legal recognition is problematic, particularly for those who begin socially and medically transitioning to their chosen gender before adulthood. These children are in the paradoxical position of being recognised as their preferred gender by bodies such as the NHS, while not being recognised by UK law. There is a risk that transgender youths will have their transgender identity exposed, and that they will be subjected to transphobic abuse.

Question 7:
Which writer does *not* reference the Equality Act?

D ✓

Question 8:
Which writer is concerned with young transgender people?

D ✓

Question 9:
Which writer mentions legislation from other countries?

B ✓

Question 10:
Which writer cites evidence from professional bodies?

C ✓

Question 11:
Which writer reports both sides of a debate about gender law reform?

A ✓

Question 12:
Which writer references empirical evidence about safeguarding concerns?

C ✓

Question 13:
Which writer supports making it easier for adults to legally declare their gender?

B

Question 14:
Which writer compares gender identification to naturalisation?

B ✓

Task Three

Read the text below, which is drawn from the introduction of a book by the art critic Walter Pater

"Many attempts have been made by writers on art and poetry to define beauty in the abstract, to express it in the most general terms, to find a universal formula for it. The value of these attempts has most often been in the suggestive and penetrating things said by the way. Such discussions help us very little to enjoy what has been well done in art or poetry, to discriminate between what is more and what is less excellent in them, or to use words like beauty, excellence, art, poetry, with a more precise meaning than they would otherwise have. Beauty, like all other qualities presented to human experience, is relative; and the definition of it becomes unmeaning and useless in proportion to its abstractness. To define beauty, not in the most abstract, but in the most concrete terms possible, to find, not a universal formula for it, but the formula which expresses most adequately this or that special manifestation of it, is the aim of the true student of aesthetics.

"To see the object as in itself it really is," has been justly said to be the aim of all true criticism whatever; and in aesthetic criticism the first step towards seeing one's object as it really is, is to know one's own impression as it really is, to discriminate it, to realise it distinctly. The objects with which aesthetic criticism deals—music, poetry, artistic and accomplished forms of human life—are indeed receptacles of so many powers or forces: they possess, like the products of nature, so many virtues or qualities. What is this song or picture, this engaging personality presented in life or in a book, to ME? What effect does it really produce on me? Does it give me pleasure? and if so, what sort or degree of pleasure? How is my nature modified by its presence, and under its influence? The answers to these questions are the original facts with which the aesthetic critic has to do; and, as in the study of light, of morals, of number, one must realise such primary data for oneself, or not at all. And he who experiences these impressions strongly, and drives directly at the discrimination and analysis of them, has no need to trouble himself with the abstract question what beauty is in itself, or what its exact relation to truth or experience—metaphysical questions, as unprofitable as metaphysical questions elsewhere. He may pass them all by as being, answerable or not, of no interest to him."

Walter Pater, *Studies in the History of the Renaissance*

Question 15:
What does the writer think is often most valuable about attempts to define beauty in the abstract?
A) These attempts result in suggestive and penetrating comments about beauty.
B) These attempts help us learn more about art and poetry.
C) Incidental comments that are not relevant to beauty per se.
D) A universal formula of beauty.

Question 16:
According to the author, what do these discussions on beauty help us with?
A) To be more precise with our aesthetic terminology.
B) To learn the difference between good and bad art.
C) To appreciate good art and poetry.
D) None of the above.

Question 17:
What does the author mean by this statement on beauty? "the definition of it becomes unmeaning and useless in proportion to its abstractness."
A) The more useless beauty is, the more meaningless its definition.
B) The more abstract the concept of beauty, the more its definition is useless.
C) The more abstract beauty becomes, the more useless it is.
D) The more abstract the definition of beauty, the more useless beauty becomes.

Question 18:

What is the aim of the true student of aesthetics, according to the author?

A) To find a useful definition of beauty.

B) To find a specific definition of beauty.

C) To find a special manifestation of beauty.

D) To find a relative definition of beauty.

Question 19:

According to the author, what do all qualities have in common?

A) They are part of human experience.

B) They are beautiful.

C) They are abstract.

D) They are subjective.

Question 20:

In paragraph 2, what must one do first in order to "see the object as in itself it really is"?

A) To see the object.

B) To know the object.

C) To know one's real impression of the object.

D) To discriminate the object distinctly.

Question 22:

In paragraph 2, what is the purpose of the writer asking questions?

A) He is listing the questions he intends to answer later in the work.

B) He is listing the questions that yield the primary data for the aesthetic critic.

C) He is listing the most important questions for the art critic to answer.

D) He is listing questions that help the art critic see the object as it really is.

Question 23:

What does the writer think about "metaphysical questions"?

A) They are not worth asking.

B) They may be answerable.

C) They may be abstract.

D) All of the above.

Question 24:

What is the writer's main aim in this passage?

A) To critique the beauty of Renaissance art.

B) To explain the true aim of the student of aesthetics when discussing beauty.

C) To criticise previous commentators on beauty.

D) To find a general definition of beauty.

Task Four

Read the text below, from an essay by the critic and poet T.S. Eliot

"The only way of expressing emotion in the form of art is by finding an "objective correlative"; in other words, a set of objects, a situation, a chain of events which shall be the formula of that particular emotion; such that when the external facts, which must terminate in sensory experience, are given, the emotion is immediately evoked. If you examine any of Shakespeare's more successful tragedies, you will find this exact equivalence; you will find that the state of mind of Lady Macbeth walking in her sleep has been communicated to you by a skilful accumulation of imagined sensory impressions; the words of Macbeth on hearing of his wife's death strike us as if, given the sequence of events, these words were automatically released by the last event in the series. The artistic "inevitability" lies in this complete adequacy of the external to the emotion; and this is precisely what is deficient in Hamlet.

Hamlet (the man) is dominated by an emotion which is inexpressible, because it is in excess of the facts as they appear. And the supposed identity of Hamlet with his author is genuine to this point: that Hamlet's bafflement at the absence of objective equivalent to his feelings is a prolongation of the bafflement of his creator in the face of his artistic problem. Hamlet is up against the difficulty that his disgust is occasioned by his mother, but that his mother is not an adequate equivalent for it; his disgust envelops and exceeds her. It is thus a feeling which he cannot understand; he cannot objectify it, and it therefore remains to poison life and obstruct action. None of the possible actions can satisfy it; and nothing that Shakespeare can do with the plot can express Hamlet for him. And it must be noticed that the very nature of the données of the problem precludes objective equivalence. To have heightened the criminality of Gertrude would have been to provide the formula for a totally different emotion in Hamlet; it is just because her character is so negative and insignificant that she arouses in Hamlet the feeling which she is incapable of representing.

The "madness" of Hamlet lay to Shakespeare's hand; in the earlier play a simple ruse, and to the end, we may presume, understood as a ruse by the audience. For Shakespeare it is less than madness and more than feigned. The levity of Hamlet, his repetition of phrase, his puns, are not part of a deliberate plan of dissimulation, but a form of emotional relief. In the character Hamlet it is the buffoonery of an emotion which can find no outlet in action; in the dramatist it is the buffoonery of an emotion which he cannot express in art. The intense feeling, ecstatic or terrible, without an object or exceeding its object, is something which every person of sensibility has known; it is doubtless a study to pathologists. It often occurs in adolescence: the ordinary person puts these feelings to sleep, or trims down his feeling to fit the business world; the artist keeps it alive by his ability to intensify the world to his emotions. The Hamlet of Laforgue is an adolescent; the Hamlet of Shakespeare is not, he has not that explanation and excuse. We must simply admit that here Shakespeare tackled a problem which proved too much for him. Why he attempted it at all is an insoluble puzzle; under compulsion of what experience he attempted to express the inexpressibly horrible, we cannot ever know. We need a great many facts in his biography; and we should like to know whether, and when, and after or at the same time as what personal experience, he read Montaigne, II. xii., Apologie de Raimond Sebond. We should have, finally, to know something which is by hypothesis unknowable, for we assume it to be an experience which, in the manner indicated, exceeded the facts. We should have to understand things which Shakespeare did not understand himself."

T.S. Eliot, *Hamlet and his Problems*

Question 25:
What does the writer mean by the term 'objective correlative?"
A) An event which is the formula for a particular emotion.
B) Objects, events or situations which are a blueprint for an emotion
C) The external facts which trigger an emotion.
D) Something which evokes an emotion.

Question 26:
What is the function of the 'objective correlative'?
A) It represents an emotion.
B) It terminates in sensory experience.
C) It evokes an emotion.
D) It is one way of expressing emotion in art.

Question 27:
According to the author, what do all of Shakespeare's most successful tragedies have in common?
A) They have an exact equivalence.
B) They contain a skilful accumulation of imagined sensory impressions.
C) The characters' mind is communicated to us.
D) They contain an 'objective correlative'

Question 28:
In paragraph one, why does the writer put the word 'inevitability' in quotation marks?
A) To express sarcasm.
B) To quote another author.
C) To signal that there isn't really any inevitability.
D) To empahsise the word.

Question 29:
In paragraph 1 and 2, what does the writer think is the main problem with the play *Hamlet*?
A) Hamlet's dominant emotion is inexpressible.
B) It is artistically inevitable.
C) The emotions are out of proportion to what is going on in the play.
D) The external is completely adequate to the emotional.

Question 30:
In paragraph 2, what does the writer claim is common between the character of Hamlet and Shakespeare?
A) They are both genuine.
B) They both suffer from artistic problems.
C) They both lack objective correlative to their emotions.
D) They are both baffled.

Question 31:
In paragraph 2, why is Hamlet's mother incapable of adequately representing Hamlet's feelings for her according to the writer?

A) Because she is not evil enough for the plot.
B) Because she is a minor character.
C) Because she is disgusting.
D) Because she is not understood by Hamlet.

Question 32:

~ 20 ~

In paragraph 3, what 'excuse' could explain Shakespeare's Hamlet according to the author.
A) If Hamlet was a buffoon.
B) If Hamlet was mad.
C) If Hamlet was a teenager.
D) If Hamlet was an artist.

Question 33:

In paragraph 3, what does the writer claim about intense feelings which exceed their object?
A) They are studied by pathologists.
B) They are ignored by ordinary people.
C) They are experienced by all sensitive people.
D) All of the above.

Question 34:

According to the author, what would we need to know before we can know why Shakespeare "tackled a problem which proved too much for him"?
A) Something which is unknowable.
B) Facts about Shakespeare's life.
C) Facts about what books he read.
D) All of the above.

Question 35:

In paragraph 3, what does the writer mean by the word 'dissimulation"?
A) Misrepresentation.
B) Madness.
C) Emotional relief.
D) Feigned.

Question 36:

What is the writer's main aim in this passage?
A) To critique the problems with *Hamlet*.
B) To explain his theory of emotion in art.
C) To discuss Shakespeare's tragedies.
D) To praise the genius of Shakespeare.

Practice Paper B

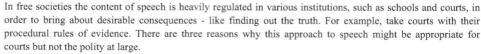

24/36

Read the two abstracts below, which summarise two academic articles on freedom of speech.

Abstract One

In free societies the content of speech is heavily regulated in various institutions, such as schools and courts, in order to bring about desirable consequences - like finding out the truth. For example, take courts with their procedural rules of evidence. There are three reasons why this approach to speech might be appropriate for courts but not the polity at large.

Firstly, the court has a reliable, reviewable, and official referee of the epistemic merits of the speech in the form of judges, while the polity does not. Secondly, only epistemic values of speech are at stake in court, whereas the polity values non-epistemic values. And thirdly, the court's jurisdiction is limited in time whereas the polity's may not be.

Only the first reason, which I call 'the problem of the epistemic arbiter, poses a serious problem for speech regulation outside institutions such as courts. I also advocate that "freedom of speech" should be regarded like "freedom of action." Speech is a human activity, and like all other human activities it can be used for good or evil; it can be harmful or beneficial; it may be helpful or destructive, and so the main issue in free speech jurisprudence should be to answer the question of how to regulate speech most effectively in order to reduce its potential harms without sacrificing its benefits. Furthermore, we should move away from fanciful rationalisations of the 'special' value of speech. I also argue against autonomy-based defences of absolute freedom of speech. The central issue in free speech jurisprudence is not really speech *per se*, but rather institutional competence. I am sceptical that capitalist democracies have the required institutional competence, but I do have some ideas about how this defect might be remedied.

Abstract Two

The American Fourteenth Amendment is committed to equality, and right by its side is the tradition of completely individual expression in the form of free speech. Libertarians advocate for absolute freedom of expression, but this can clash with the goal of equality if hate speech is allowed. Even though the US government has no power to treat the speech of similar persons differently, interpersonal conflict can occur when the personal safety or rights of one individual is threatened by the free speech of another. New challenges frequently arise due to the expansion of the internet, because hate speech transmitted from the USA has global reach. Propaganda which is legal in the United States may be streamed into other countries, such as France, where such speech constitutes a criminal offence.

World democracies are challenged by the global reach of racist ideology. Societies which are committed to pluralism have to promote egalitarian principles against harming others' dignity while also safeguarding personal expression. This means that even though America lauds freedom of speech, there are many cases in which public communications are restrained in order to promote competing interests, such as preserving one's good reputation. If one person desires to say false things about another, defamation law protects personal reputation and not speech. In this case, we prioritise a person's right to protect his own good name – this "reflects no more than our basic concept of the essential dignity and worth of every human being." The interests of libelled people are favoured, for reasons of public policy, over the interest of those who want to intentionally or carelessly spread falsehoods.

A similar approach can be seen in cases where words are likely to breach the peace. The Supreme Court has found that there is a higher social interest in maintaining order and morals that justifies at least some limitations on free speech.

Question 1:

What view of free speech is advocated by the writer of abstract 1?

A) Free speech has a special value.

B) The court's approach to free speech should be adopted generally.

C) Speech should be treated similarly to action.

D) Speech should be absolutely free in the interests of autonomy.

Question 2:

In abstract 1, what does the author identify as the *main problem* for speech regulation in the polity?

A) The polity's jurisdiction is unlimited.

B) Capitalist democracies lack institutional competence.

C) The polity lacks an official referee of the epistemic merits off speech.

D) The polity values non-epistemic values and not just epistemic ones.

Question 3:

In abstract 2, in what situation would a restriction of speech be most likely unjustified according to the author?

A) Damaging another person's reputation by spreading falsehoods.

B) Spreading Libertarian ideas.

C) Communicating racist propaganda online. B

D) Breaching the peace.

Question 4:

According to the author of abstract 2 free speech may conflict with what?

A) The Fourteenth Amendment.

B) Racist ideology.

C) Hate speech.

D) The goals of equality.

Question 5:

Which abstract or abstracts assume that freedom of speech should be absolute?

A) Neither abstract

B) Both abstracts

C) Abstract One only

D) Abstract Two only

Question 6:

Which abstract discusses the regulation of speech in the context of the institution of the court?

A) Neither abstract

B) Both abstracts

C) Abstract One only

D) Abstract Two only

Task Two

Read the four texts below, which give the views of four writers on the idea of changing the voting age.

A) Molly Scott Cato

Elections allow us to decide the future of Britain, so it's really important that young people get to have their say about which direction the country should take. We need to allow 16-year olds to vote now. When you hit 16 you must pay taxes, you can join the military, you can legally leave home, and you can even get married. If you can do all of these things, then there is no good reason why you shouldn't also be allowed to vote. At age 16 you are entitled to have a say about your country's future, and you are entitled to have a say about issues which affect your daily life.

B) David Runciman

Lowering the voting age to 16 doesn't go far enough: I would lower it to 6. I'm not joking. People who are able to read should be able to vote, so that would exclude very young children. What could go wrong? It would be fun and would make elections more interesting. Of course, it's never going to happen, but if you want to illustrate how out of kilter our democracies have become why shouldn't 6-year olds get the vote?

The elderly, as a group, have a massive advantage in representative democracies. Young people are seriously outnumbered because the voting age is restricted to 18, whereas there isn't a cap on voting age at the other end. 75-year olds don't lose the right to vote. You can continue to vote until the day you die, and there is no competency test. You could have severe dementia and still be allowed to vote, which is quite right. But young people are losing out.

C) Bryan Caplan

Forget about special interest groups, or excessive lobbying: the irrationality, biases, and misconceived beliefs of ordinary voters is the greatest obstacle to sound economic policy. Time and time again Voters elect politicians who claim to share their biases, which results in poor economic policies winning by popular demand.

Voters are biased in four ways: they don't trust the mechanism of the market, they dislike foreigners, they underestimate the value of conserving labour, and they are pessimists who believe the market is going to get worse and worse. The markets should be empowered to pick up the slack: democracies should do less.

D) Tyler Cowen

Most of what we do in life is for the purpose of expressing our values, so you shouldn't feel guilty about voting (if you even vote!) People who believe they are being rational by refusing to vote are the most deceived. They are actually engaging in a less transparent form of expression (which is a protest against voting) but disguise that expressive behaviour as a kind of rationality. The best argument against voting is this: don't vote if you don't like it, or if you don't know which candidate to choose. High-status people hardly ever admit to not knowing which candidate is better, even though the extent of disagreement among high-status people suggest that they don't really know which candidate is best.

In other words, the act of voting and not voting are both motivated by the idea that you are better than other people. And I am really glad that we have a whole day devoted to this important idea.

Question 7:
Which writer suggests that voting is an expressive activity?

D ✓

Question 8:
Which writer has the biggest concern with economics?

C ✓

Question 9:
Which writer gives an example of a change to voting that is intended to strike the reader as absurd?

B ✓

Question 10:
Which writer gives concrete reasons why the voting age should be lowered to 16?

A ✓

Question 11:
Which writer has a pessimistic view about voters' capabilities?

A C ✓

Question 12:
Which writer has a sarcastic attitude towards the concept of elections and voting in general?

B ✗

Question 13:
Which writer focuses on a generational clash?

B ✓

Question 14:
Which writer gives an argument against voting?

D ✓

Task Three

Read the text below, by the French philosopher Voltaire.

The members of the English Parliament are fond of comparing themselves to the old Romans. Not long since Mr. Shippen opened a speech in the House of Commons with these words, "The majesty of the people of England would be wounded." The singularity of the expression occasioned a loud laugh; but this gentleman, so far from being disconcerted, repeated the same words with a resolute tone of voice, and the laugh ceased.

In my opinion, the majesty of the people of England has nothing in common with that of the people of Rome, much less is there any affinity between their Governments. There is in London a senate, some of the members whereof are accused (doubtless very unjustly) of selling their voices on certain occasions, as was done in Rome; this is the only resemblance. Besides, the two nations appear to me quite opposite in character, with regard both to good and evil. The Romans never knew the dreadful folly of religious wars, an abomination reserved for devout preachers of patience and humility. Marious and Sylla, Cæsar and Pompey, Anthony and Augustus, did not draw their swords and set the world in a blaze merely to determine whether the flamen should wear his shirt over his robe, or his robe over his shirt, or whether the sacred chickens should eat and drink, or eat only, in order to take the augury. The English have hanged one another by law, and cut one another to pieces in pitched battles, for quarrels of as trifling nature. The sects of the Episcopalians and Presbyterians quite distracted these very serious heads for a time. But I fancy they will hardly ever be so silly again, they seeming to be grown wiser at their own expense; and I do not perceive the least inclination in them to murder one another merely about syllogisms, as some zealots among them once did.

But here follows a more essential difference between Rome and England, which gives the advantage entirely to the later—viz., that the civil wars of Rome ended in slavery, and those of the English in liberty. The English are the only people upon earth who have been able to prescribe limits to the power of kings by resisting them; and who, by a series of struggles, have at last established that wise Government where the Prince is all powerful to do good, and, at the same time, is restrained from committing evil; where the nobles are great without insolence, though there are no vassals; and where the people share in the Government without confusion.

The House of Lords and that of the Commons divide the legislative power under the king, but the Romans had no such balance. The patricians and plebeians in Rome were perpetually at variance, and there was no intermediate power to reconcile them. The Roman senate, who were so unjustly, so criminally proud as not to suffer the plebeians to share with them in anything, could find no other artifice to keep the latter out of the administration than by employing them in foreign wars. They considered the plebeians as a wild beast, whom it behoved them to let loose upon their neighbours, for fear they should devour their masters. Thus the greatest defect in the Government of the Romans raised them to be conquerors. By being unhappy at home, they triumphed over and possessed themselves of the world, till at last their divisions sunk them to slavery.

The Government of England will never rise to so exalted a pitch of glory, nor will its end be so fatal. The English are not fired with the splendid folly of making conquests, but would only prevent their neighbours from conquering. They are not only jealous of their own liberty, but even of that of other nations. The English were exasperated against Louis XIV. for no other reason but because he was ambitious, and declared war against him merely out of levity, not from any interested motives.

Letters on the English, Voltaire

Question 15:

What is the only similarity between the Romans and the English, according to the author?

A) None.

B) They have similar ideas about good and evil.

C) They both have a senate.

D) The representatives are sometimes accused of bribery.

Question 16:

What is the author's attitude towards disputes over "whether the flamen should wear his shirt over his robe, or his robe over his shirt, or whether the sacred chickens should eat and drink?"

A) They are serious.

B) They are abominable.

C) They are trivial.

D) They are a folly.

Question 17:

Why does the author think there won't be another religious war in England?

A) The English no longer have quarrels of a trifling nature.

B) The religious sects don't care about syllogisms any more.

C) The Presbyterians and the Episcopalians aren't silly.

D) The religious sects have learned their lesson after suffering losses in previous wars.

Question 18:

Which of the following is *not* a feature of the English Government, according to the author?

A) The King has unlimited power.

B) The King is restrained from committing evil.

C) There are no serfs.

D) The people participate in the government.

Question 19:

According to the author, how did the patricians keep the plebians away from power?

A) The patricians enslaved the plebians.

B) The plebians and patricians were perpetually at variance with each other.

C) The patricians sent the plebians to fight in conflicts.

D) The plebians divided the legislative power to restore balance.

Question 20:

The author implies that the conflict between the patricians and the plebians could be resolved by...

A) Making the senate less proud and selfish.

B) Installing a third branch of government.

C) The plebians taking power for themselves.

D) Installing a House of Lords, and a House of Commons, like in England.

Question 21:

In the final paragraph, what does the author mean when he states that the English declared war on France "out of levity"?

A) England felt duty-bound to declare war.

B) England was serious about declaring war.

C) England was ambitious in declaring war.

D) England was flippant in declaring war.

Question 22:
Why will England never be as glorious as Rome, according to the author?
A) England doesn't like to conquer other nations.
B) England wants other nations to be free.
C) England is deeply concerned with remaining free.
D) All of the above.

Question 23:
According to the author, why did the Romans eventually descend into slavery?
A) The Romans were too conflicted with each other.
B) The Romans fought too many conquests abroad.
C) The Romans were unhappy at home.
D) The Romans were undemocratic.

Question 24:
What is the writer's main aim in this extract?
A) To explain why the English will never be as great as the Romans.
B) To compare the similarities and differences between two cultures.
C) To explain why the English will never have another religious war.
D) To explain how the Romans sunk into slavery.

Task Four

Read the text below, taken from a book by the American writer and thinker Ralph Waldo Emerson.

Of British universities, Cambridge has the most illustrious names on its list. At the present day, too, it has the advantage of Oxford, counting in its alumni a greater number of distinguished scholars. I regret that I had but a single day wherein to see King's College Chapel, the beautiful lawns and gardens of the colleges, and a few of its gownsmen.

But I availed myself of some repeated invitations to Oxford, where I had introductions to Dr. Daubeny, Professor of Botany, and to the Regius Professor of Divinity, as well as to a valued friend, a fellow of Oriel, and went thither on the last day of March, 1848. I was the guest of my friend in Oriel, was housed close upon that college, and I lived on college hospitalities.

My new friends showed me their cloisters, the Bodleian Library, the Randolph Gallery, Merton Hall, and the rest. I saw several faithful high-minded young men, some of them in the mood of making sacrifices for peace of mind,—a topic, of course, on which I had no counsel to offer. Their affectionate and gregarious ways reminded me at once of the habits of our Cambridge men, though I imputed to these English an advantage in their secure and polished manners.

The halls are rich with oaken wainscoting and ceiling. The pictures of the founders hang from the walls; the tables glitter with plate. A youth came forward to the upper table, and pronounced the ancient form of grace before meals, which, I suppose, has been in use here for ages, Benedictus benedicat; benedicitur, benedicatur.

It is a curious proof of the English use and wont, or of their good nature, that these young men are locked up every night at nine o'clock, and the porter at each hall is required to give the name of any belated student who is admitted after that hour. Still more descriptive is the fact that out of twelve hundred young men, comprising the most spirited of the aristocracy, a duel has never occurred.

English Traits: Universities, Ralph Waldo Emerson

Question 25:

Why is Cambridge superior to Oxford, according to the author?

A) It has the most illustrious names.

B) It has a greater number of distinguished scholars.   ✗

C) It has a greater number of distinguished alumni.

D) It has the advantage of Oxford.

Question 26:

Which of the below did Emerson not meet during his visit?

A) A fellow of Oriel

B) A student of botany

C) A professor of divinity   ✓

D) A professor of botany

Question 27:

Where did the author visit during his stay in Oxford?   ✓

A) Merton Hall, the Bodleian Library, the cloisters.

B) The Bodleian Library, the Randolph Gallery, Merton Hall, the gardens.

C) The Randolph Gallery, Merton Hall, the cloisters, The Bodleian Library.

D) The Randolph Gallery, the cloisters, The Bodleian Library.

Question 28:

In paragraph 3, why does the author "of course" have no counsel to offer the "faithful, high-minded young men"?

A) He doesn't know anything about the topic of sacrifice for peace of mind.

B) He doesn't want to offer the men advice.

C) He isn't in the mood to offer counsel.

D) The text doesn't give enough information to say.

Question 29:

What best describes the character of the Oxford men, according to the author?

A) Well-mannered.

B) Sacrificial.

C) Loving and sociable.   ✗

D) Contended.

Question 30:

What summarises the author's views most accurately?

A) Cambridge men aren't as affectionate as Oxford men.

B) Cambridge men have better manners than Oxford men.

C) Cambridge men are more affectionate than Oxford men.   ✓

D) Cambridge men are less polished than Oxford men.

Question 31:

In paragraph 4, the author describes dinner at formal hall. What is his main aim in describing this scene?

A) To convey a light-hearted event in a humorous way.

B) To emphasise the solemnity and sense of history.

C) To convey nostalgia.

D) To poke fun at the seriousness of the situation.

Question 32:

What does the phrase "use and wont" mean?

A) Character

B) Good nature

C) Personality

D) Custom

Question 33:

What does the author cite as the main evidence that the English are good natured?

A) The porter has to take the names of late students.

B) A duel has never occurred amongst the students.

C) The students are locked up at nine.

D) The students are spirited young aristocrats.

Question 34:

Does the author personally prefer Oxford or Cambridge?

A) Oxford

B)Cambridge

C) Both

D) Can't tell

Question 35:

Which word best describes the author's attitude towards the English?

A) Positive

B) Contemptuous

C) Worshipful

D) Confused

Question 36:

What is the author's goal in this passage?

A) To contrast Oxford and Cambridge

B) To critique the backward ways of the old world

C) To offer his thoughts on the character of the English

D) To praise the superiority of English universities over American.

Practice Paper C

Task One

Read the two abstracts below, which summarise two academic articles on military conscription.

Abstract One

In this paper I use cross-country data to study what determines whether a country elects to conscript its military forces. I focus on factors such as the ready supply of young males, the nature of the political regime, the legal institutions, military threat, and economic power, in the decision to conscript. Democracies with larger populations than neighbouring countries (which I infer to present a lesser threat) are less likely to conscript than dictatorships. But when I examine the effect that threat has on each type of regime, I discover that the effect of threat is not a significant factor in explaining the existence of conscription policies. What, then, accounts for the extent of conscription? I find that the size of the military relative to the population is unaffected by increased threat in countries that elect to conscript. Countries with volunteer forces have larger militaries when increased threat is present. In a sample which contains conscripted and non-conscripted countries, the size of the military increases in proportion to the increase of threat, regardless of whether the country is democratic. I also find that countries with British legal origins are less likely to conscript, while countries with Soviet legal origins are more likely; and countries with higher proportions of young males are also more likely to conscript.

Abstract Two

One popular justification for conscription is that it limits support for war by radically changing the identities of those who would suffer the cost of fighting a nation's wars. If the military is conscripted there is a much higher chance that the offspring of richer and politically well-connected people will serve in the armed forces, which gives these people a strong incentive to campaign against war.

However, the problem with this argument is that it ignores the fact that avoiding war for a nation is a wider public good, and so is subject to the classic problem of the free-rider. We develop a model to demonstrate that the under-provision of anti-war campaigning from those who wish to avoid the draft is made worse by the fact that seeking deferment provides a superior private benefit. Resources that a rich or politically powerful individual devotes to stopping a war will not be very likely to have any noticeable effect on the outcome. In comparison, resources that are spent to guarantee deferment or a non-combat role for a family member have a potent, direct effect on a private good. The effectiveness of using the draft as a means of reducing political support for war, when compared to an all-volunteer force, is limited. Empirical findings from the Vietnam War are also consistent with our thesis.

Question 1:
What inference does the writer claim to make in abstract one?
A) Democracies with large populations present less of a threat.
B) Democracies are less likely to conscript than dictatorships.
C) Neighbouring countries with smaller populations present less of a threat to democracies.
D) Neighbouring countries with smaller populations present less of a threat to dictatorships.

Question 2:

In abstract one, what claim does the author make?

A) When threat is present, countries with volunteer forces have smaller militaries.

B) When threat is present, countries with conscription forces have larger militaries.

C) When threat is present, countries with conscription forces have smaller militaries.

D) When threat is present, countries with volunteer forces have larger militaries.

Question 3:

According to abstract 2, what assumption does the author make about the 'popular justification' for conscription.

A) Poor working-class people are less able to campaign effectively against wars.

B) The offspring of rich and well-connected people are better fighters than poor working-class people.

C) The offspring of rich and well-connected people will like to fight in the wars.

D) The offspring of rich and well-connected people will be more likely to serve in the armed forces.

Question 4:

According to abstract two, what does the author's model predict in the event of conscription?

A) Resources spent to stop the war will be highly effective, and resources spent to get a loved one out of the draft will also be effective.

B) Resources spent to stop the war will be highly effective, and resources spent to get a loved out out of the draft will have little effect.

C) Resources spent to stop the war will have very little effect, whereas resources spent to get a loved one out of the draft will be very effective.

D) Resources spent to stop the war will have very little effect, and resources spent to get a loved one out of the draft will also have little impact.

Question 5:

Which abstract presents an argument for or against conscription?

A) Neither abstract

B) Both abstracts

C) Abstract one only

D) Abstract two only

Question 6:

Which abstract references empirical evidence?

A) Neither abstracts

B) Both Abstracts

C) Abstract one only

D) Abstract two only

Task Two

Read the four texts below, which give the views of four academic writers on raising the minimum wage

A) Mitch Downey
Current research suggests that technological advances exert pressure on middle-wage occupations because routine tasks are automatized. I argue that these tasks are not fully automated by technology – very often, they still require some labour. Rather, technology enables less skilled workers to perform the same job by reducing task complexity. The cost of automation includes not only the cost of the technology itself, but also the cost of the low-wage workers who will use it. If we raise the cost of low-wage labour, the minimum wage will reduce the profitability of adopting automating technologies.

B) Alex Tabbarok
Amazon's recently increased minimum wage coincided with the end of the monthly bonus plan, which could add 8% to a worker's salary (and up to 16% during the holidays), and its stock share program which gave workers shares worth almost four thousand dollars when they hit two years of employment with the company. It's looking like most workers will still gain an overall benefit, due to the tightness of the labour market, but the lauded increase in minimum wage is not as generous as it first seemed.

What can minimum wage researchers learn from this? Amazon freely opted to increase its wages, but what if they had been mandated to increase the minimum wage by law? What would Amazon have done then? It seems obvious that Amazon, at the very least, would have ended the bonus plan and the stock share program. In this situation, the increase in minimum wage would not lower employment very much. One might conclude, in such a situation, that minimum wage increases do not reduce employment because the demand for labour is inelastic. This reasoning is fallacious, but the conclusion is right. The correct analysis is that the minimum wage didn't reduce employment simply because the minimum wage didn't increase overall wages that much.

C)Paul de Grauwe
During the past few decades in the UK, income distribution has seriously deteriorated. An increasing proportion of economic growth has been taken by the top 10 percent of the population. This massive increase in inequality results in more extreme political movements and undermines the social agreement in the market system.
A minimum wage helps to combat rising inequality. In the long run, it will make capitalism more sustainable. It will show a more human, caring face of capitalism. And overall it will strengthen the economic system.

D)Stephen Wright
When it comes to eliminating poverty, wages are a crude instrument (but not as crude as universal benefits for pensioners)…A living wage, built around consumption needs, is not logical. If it has any rational basis at all, there should be a set of living wages which apply to different household types.

I personally think that reduction of poverty for those who work should be carried out via benefit policies. One of Gordon Brown's greatest unheard successes was the tax credit system. I'm confident that this system is the primary reason for our continual low unemployment rate, and the resilience of employment during the recent recession. It would be a pity to discard it just when it has really shown how valuable it is.

Question 7:

Which writer suggests that minimum wage will combat inequality?

C

Question 8:

Which writer disputes the standard view of automation?

A

Question 9:

Which writer advocates government benefits as opposed to minimum wage increases?

D

Question 10:

Which writer rejects the one size fits all model of the minimum wage?

B

Question 11:

Which writer corrects an invalid argument about minimum wage increases?

A

Question 12:

Which writer gives several tangible benefits of the minimum wage?

C

Question 13:

Which writer references a recent event?

B

Question 14:

Which writer advocates a reduction in poverty?

D

Task Three

Read the text below, by the English philosopher John Locke.

A sound mind in a sound body, is a short, but full description of a happy state in this world. He that has these two, has little more to wish for; and he that wants either of them, will be but little the better for any thing else. Men's happiness or misery is most part of their own making. He, whose mind directs not wisely, will never take the right way; and he, whose body is crazy and feeble, will never be able to advance in it.

 I confess, there are some men's constitutions of body and mind so vigorous, and well fram'd by nature, that they need not much assistance from others; but by the strength of their natural genius, they are from their cradles carried towards what is excellent; and by the privilege of their happy constitutions, are able to do wonders. But examples of this kind are but few; and I think I may say, that of all the men we meet with, nine parts of ten are what they are, good or evil, useful or not, by their education. 'Tis that which makes the great difference in mankind. The little, or almost insensible impressions on our tender infancies, have very important and lasting consequences: and there 'tis, as in the fountains of some rivers, where a gentle application of the hand turns the flexible waters in channels, that make them take quite contrary courses; and by this direction given them at first in the source, they receive different tendencies, and arrive at last at very remote and distant places.

I imagine the minds of children as easily turn'd this or that way, as water itself: and though this be the principal part, and our main care should be about the inside, yet the clay-cottage is not to be neglected. I shall therefore begin with the case, and consider first the health of the body, as that which perhaps you may rather expect from that study I have been thought more peculiarly to have apply'd my self to; and that also which will be soonest dispatch'd, as lying, if I guess not amiss, in a very little compass.

How necessary health is to our business and happiness; and how requisite a strong constitution, able to endure hardships and fatigue, is to one that will make any figure in the world, is too obvious to need any proof.

Some Thoughts Concerning Education, John Locke

Question 15:

What claim does the writer make about "a sound mind in a sound body?"

A) A person who has these will only need to wish for a little bit more to be happy.
B) A person who desires these things will be benefited by them the most.
C) A person who lacks these things will not be benefited much if he gains them.
D) A person who has these will not need much else to be happy.

Question 16:

Based on paragraph 1, what statement would the author most disagree with?
A) Happiness is entirely all about having a healthy body and mind.
B) How our lives go is wholly out of our control.
C) Only wise people can make good choices.
D) A person with a sick body will not be able to advance in it.

Question 17:

What does the writer mean by humans who are 'well fram'd by nature' in paragraph 2?
A) Some humans are naturally beautiful.
B) Some humans learn to develop their minds and strengthen their bodies.
C) Some humans don't need assistance from others.
D) Some humans are born with vigorous bodies and minds.

Question 18:

What has the largest impact on a human's character, according to the author?
A) Nature.
B) A healthy mind and healthy body.
C) Education.
D) Our own choices.

Question 19:

What point is the author trying to convey with his river metaphor in paragraph 2?
A) Human life fluid and flowing, like a river.
B) Education is like a river that we float on.
C) The smallest cause can have a massive effect on our lives.
D) Education is like a river that can take us to distant lands.

Question 20:

In paragraph 3 what does the 'clay-cottage' refer to?
A) Cottages by a river.
B) The mind.
C) Education.
D) The body

Question 21:
What word best describes the minds of children, according to the author?
A) Irrational.
B) Vacillating.
C) Flowing.
D) Constant.

Question 22:
What premise is so obvious to the author that he claims he doesn't need to provide an argument for it?
A) That education contributes 9/10 to who we are.
B) That human happiness is mostly of our own making.
C) That a healthy body is necessary for happiness.
D) That insensible impressions during our childhood have lasting effects.

Question 23:
What does the writer mean when he describes the topic of health of the body as "that also which will be soonest dispatch'd, as lying, if I guess not amiss, in a very little compass."
A) He is lying when he discusses the topic of bodily health.
B) The topic of bodily health is akin to a compass.
C) The topic of bodily health can be discussed and set aside very briefly.
D) The topic of bodily health will be dealt with first.

Question 24:
What best describes the writer's main aim in this extract?
A) To discuss the cultivation of body and mind.
B) To discuss the workings of the mind.
C) To discuss happiness.
D) To discuss natural geniuses.

Task Four

Read the text below, by the American writer Emily Post.

So long as Romance exists and Lochinvar(1) remains young manhood's ideal, love at first sight and marriage in a week is within the boundaries of possibility. But usually (and certainly more wisely) a young man is for some time attentive to a young woman before dreaming of marriage. Thus not only have her parents plenty of time to find out what manner of man he is, and either accept or take means to prevent a serious situation; but the modern young woman herself is not likely to be "carried away" by the personality of anyone whose character and temperament she does not pretty thoroughly understand and weigh.

In nothing does the present time more greatly differ from the close of the last century, than in the unreserved frankness of young women and men towards each other. Those who speak of the domination of sex in this day are either too young to remember, or else have not stopped to consider, that mystery played a far greater and more dangerous role when sex, like a woman's ankle, was carefully hidden from view, and therefore far more alluring than to-day when both are commonplace matters.

In cities twenty-five years ago, a young girl had beaux who came to see her one at a time; they in formal clothes and manners, she in her "company best" to "receive" them, sat stiffly in the "front parlor" and made politely formal conversation. Invariably they addressed each other as Miss Smith and Mr. Jones, and they "talked off the top" with about the same lack of reservation as the ambassador of one country may be supposed to talk to him of another. A young man was said to be "devoted" to this young girl or that, but as a matter of fact each was acting a role, he of an admirer and she of a siren, and each was actually an utter stranger to the other.

To-day no trace of stilted artificiality remains. The tête-a-tête of a quarter of a century ago has given place to the continual presence of a group. A flock of young girls and a flock of young men form a little group of their own—everywhere they are together. In the country they visit the same houses or they live in the same neighborhood, they play golf in foursomes, and tennis in mixed doubles. In winter at balls they sit at the same table for supper, they have little dances at their own homes, where scarcely any but themselves are invited; they play bridge, they have tea together, but whatever they do, they stay in the pack.

In more than one way this group habit is excellent; young women and men are friends in a degree of natural and entirely platonic intimacy undreamed of in their parents' youth. Having the habit therefore of knowing her men friends well, a young girl is not going to imagine a stranger, no matter how perfect he may appear to be, anything but an ordinary human man after all. And in finding out his bad points as well as his good, she is aided and abetted, encouraged or held in check, by the members of the group to which she belongs.

Etiquette: Engagements, Emily Post

(1) Lochinvar is the handsome and knightly hero of a romantic poem by Sir Walter Scott of the same name. He embodies the traditional virtues of manhood.

Question 25:

Why does the writer think it is more usual for marriages to take place after a period of courtship?

A) Young women of today are less likely to get carried away.

B) It is preferable for the young woman's family to get to know the man first.

C) Love at first sight is possible, but far less likely.

D) All of the above.

Question 26:

When would weddings within a week no longer be a possibility, according to the writer?

A) If there was no love at first sight.

B) If Lochnivar remained young manhood's ideal.

C) If young men were attentive to one woman for a time before marriage.

D) If Romance didn't exist and if Lochnivar was not manhood's ideal.

Question 27:

What is the purpose of the comparison between sex and ankles in paragraph 2?

A) To illustrate that women are much less modest than they used to be.

B) To illustrate the change in female fashion since the turn of the century.

C) To illustrate that both sex and ankles have become less hidden from view.

D) To illustrate that sex and ankles are both alluring.

Question 28:

What is the biggest difference between the turn of the century and the time the author is writing in?

A) Sex is less mysterious.

B) Men and women are more open with each other.

C) Women are wearing less restrictive fashions.

D) Men and women are less honest with each other.

(the biggest difference is the "unreserved frankness" between men and women. This means they are more open with each other.)

Question 29:

In paragraph 3, What effect does the writer convey by putting the words "company best", "receive", and "front parlor" in quotation marks?

A) To emphasise, and poke fun, of the stuffy etiquette of dating in the past.

B) To express sarcasm.

C) To express disagreement with the dating conventions of the past.

D) To signal that she is quoting someone else.

Question 30:

In paragraph 3, which word best describes the writer's attitude towards the young man's "devotion"?

A) Admiring.

B) Sceptical.

C) Wistful.

D) Contemptuous.

Question 31:

What word best describes the dating convention in the writer's day as opposed to the convention described in paragraph 3?

A) Formal.
B) Stilted.
C) Authentic.
D) Artificial.

Question 32:

In paragraph 4, what activity does the writer *not* mention the groups taking part in?

A) Having supper together.
B) Dancing at balls.
C) Having tea.
D) Visiting homes.

Question 33:

In paragraph 5, which of the following is *not* a reason why the group habit is "excellent"?

A) Young women are free to be friends with young men in a way that was never possible for their parents.
B) Young women are less likely to be dazzled by seemingly perfect strangers.
C) The group can guide and advise each other in matters of love.
D) Young women will find love with one of their male friends.

Question 34:

What does the word 'platonic' mean in the context of paragraph 5?

A) Natural.
B) Romantic.
C) Intimate.
D) Friendly.

Question 35:

Based on your impression of the overall passage, which scenario would the writer most likely approve of the most?

A) A woman marrying a young man after one romantic week.
B) A woman marrying one of her young male friends.
C) A woman marrying a man after courting him in the style of 25 years ago.
D) A young woman marrying a man she had just met who she thought was perfect.

Question 36:

What is the writer's overall aim in this passage?

A) To discuss the changes in courtship and attitudes towards engagement.
B) To advise how to go on dates.
C) To criticise the conventions of the past.
D) To criticise the lack of decorum between men and women.

Practice Paper D

28/20

Task One

Read the two abstracts below, which summarise two academic articles on the idea of surveillance capitalism.

Abstract One

In this article, I describe 'surveillance capitalism' and consider its implications for 'information civilisation.' Google is to surveillance capitalism as Ford is to mass assembly, so the practices and assumptions of Google Inc. as presented in two recent articles written by Google's chief economist Hal Varian are the focal lens for my analysis. Varian postulates four uses that derive from computer-mediated transactions: 'data extraction and analysis; 'better monitoring resulting in new contractual forms', 'customisation and personalisation', and 'continuous experiments'. An analysis of the properties and effects of these uses reveals the innate logic of surveillance capitalism and the framework of computer mediation upon which it depends. This framework, or architecture, creates a distributed new kind of power that I call 'Big other'. It is characterised by unpredictable and often inscrutable mechanisms of extraction, control, and commodification that effectively distances people from their own behaviours while producing new markets of behavioural modification and prediction. Surveillance capitalism challenges democratic values and deviates in crucial ways from the decades long evolution of market capitalism.

Abstract Two

This paper argues that the United States is reinventing colonialism in the Global South via its supremacy over digital technology, and it proposes an explanatory framework for this phenomenon. Using South Africa as an example, it argues that the USA exercises colonial control at the architecture level of the digital ecosystem which encompasses hardware, software, and network connectivity.

This control results in five kinds of domination. Firstly, there is a new form of economic domination: the monopoly powers of multinational companies extract resources through digital surveillance and rent. Secondly, through their control of the digital ecosystem Big Tech corporations control computer-mediated interfaces, which gives them direct influence over economic, cultural and political aspects of life. This is a new form of imperial control. Thirdly, the core of surveillance capitalism is Big Data, which violates people's privacy and loads economic power into the hands of US companies – a kind of global surveillance capitalism. Fourthly, Global North intelligence agencies work with corporations to conduct surveillance, both mass and targeted, in the Global South. This increases imperial state surveillance. Fifthly, the USA has persuaded people that society must go along with its own elitist ideas of the digital world, which sets up the foundations for a kind of tech hegemony.

Question 1:
Why does the writer of abstract one compare Google to Ford? ("Google is to surveillance capitalism as Ford is to mass assembly")
A) To emphasise that both are large American companies.
B) To emphasise that Google is associated with surveillance capitalism.
C) To emphasise that both companies are leaders in their paradigm fields of expertise.
D) To emphasise that Google mass assembles surveillance capitalism.

Question 2:

According to the writer of abstract one, which of the following is a feature of 'the Big Other'?

A) It capitalises on behavioural forecasts.

B) It is opaque and unpredictable.

C) It alienates people from their own actions.

D) All of the above.

Question 3:

Which of the following is not a kind of domination, according to the writer of abstract two?

A) Tech domination.

B) Service domination.

C) Cultural domination.

D) Economic domination.

Question 4:

According to the writer of abstract 2, how is the USA reinventing colonialism in the global South??

A) Via control of digital technology.

B) Via hardware and software.

C) Via economic domination.

D) Via surveillance capitalism.

Question 5:

Which abstract or abstracts welcomes the idea of surveillance capitalism?

A) Neither abstract.

B) Both abstracts.

C) Abstract One only.

D) Abstract Two only.

Question 6:

Which article or articles is concerned with the system of control that stems from surveillance capitalism?

A) Neither abstract.

B) Both abstracts.

C) Abstract One Only.

D) Abstract Two only.

Task Two
Read the four texts below, which give the views of four academic writers on the ethics of borders and migration.

A) Robert Shiller

In the last few hundred years, there have been a series of intellectual revolutions against oppression. These revolutions are not globally propagated by war (which involves multiple causes), but by communication and language technology. Ultimately, the ideas of these revolutions become uncontroversial – unlike the causes of war.

The next intellectual revolution, which will probably occur at some point in the 21st Century, will challenge the economic consequences of the nation-state. It will focus on the unfairness that, entirely by luck, some people are born in prosperous countries and others are born in poor countries. As more and more people work for international firms, and get to know individuals from other countries, our sense of justice will change.

B) Alex Tabbarok

Governments should protect the basic liberty of freedom of movement unless there are reasonable extenuating circumstances. This should extend to movement across international borders.

Domestic and international laws already acknowledge the right of individuals to leave their countries. This right of movement may only be limited in extreme circumstances in which public safety is imminently threatened.
I believe that international and domestic laws should extend this protection to people who wish to enter another country. Although there may be occasions when governments are justified in treating foreigners differently from domestic citizens, freedom of movement and residence are basic rights that should only be limited when it is absolutely necessary.

C) Tyler Cowen

When it comes to immigration policies, land-use restrictions are more important than border control. The key factor is not just how many people can get into the country, but who can afford to live here. Of relevance is zoning laws, policies about squatters, rules for homesteading public property, and how many people are permitted to live in a single apartment. When I use the term 'open borders' this also encompasses liberal land use policies. Open border policies would not really matter if unskilled workers couldn't also afford to reside in the USA. (And for the anti-immigration types – you concentrate too much on how easy it is to cross the border, and not nearly enough on how much it costs to live here. The extent to which the best immigration restrictions involve land use policy or border policy is an underexplored topic.)

If the border and the land use were both free, markets would be a powerful force in organising mass migration. Take, for example, Hyderabad in India. A significant number of the poorest citizens live on garbage dumps: they live in tents and derelict huts. Every day they search the garbage dump for useful items. Why do these people live there? Is it because they like the short distance to work? Is it because they enjoy the culture of the garbage dump? Absolutely not. These people live there because they want to have a chance of survival.

D) Jonathan Adler

Restrictions on migration, like any other government power, can be abused. However, just because specific immigration policies are bad does not mean that the whole enterprise of policing borders is bad.
A foundational principle of national sovereignty is control over the nation's territory, including the borders. The very thing that makes a nation sovereign is that the government has power and responsibility for its territory. This entails that the government has the authority to exclude outsiders.

Question 7:

Which writer thinks that migration is a basic human right?

Question 8:

Which writer thinks that border control is necessary for a free nation?

Question 9:

Which writer postulates that our ideas about immigration will radically change in the future?

Question 10:

Which writer takes an historical approach?

Question 11:

Which writer addresses people who are critical of open border policies?

Question 12:

Which writer thinks that the emphasis on border control is misplaced?

Question 13:

Which writer hypothesises that more people will eventually work for global firms?

Question 14:

Which writer thinks that tough immigration control is permissible?

Task Three

Read the text below, by the English political theorist Edmund Burke.

It is thus in real calamities. In imitated distresses the only difference is the pleasure resulting from the effects of imitation; for it is never so perfect, but we can perceive it is imitation, and on that principle are somewhat pleased with it. And indeed in some cases we derive as much or more pleasure from that source than from the thing itself. But then I imagine we shall be much mistaken, if we attribute any considerable part of our satisfaction in tragedy to the consideration that tragedy is a deceit, and its representations no realities. The nearer it approaches the reality, and the farther it removes us from all idea of fiction, the more perfect is its power. But be its power of what kind it will, it never approaches to what it represents. Choose a day on which to represent the most sublime and affecting tragedy we have; appoint the most favourite actors; spare no cost upon the scenes and decorations, unite the greatest efforts of poetry, painting, and music; and when you have collected your audience, just at the moment when their minds are erect with expectation, let it be reported that a state criminal of high rank is on the point of being executed in the adjoining square; in a moment the emptiness of the theatre would demonstrate the comparative weakness of the imitative arts, and proclaim the triumph of the real sympathy.

I believe that this notion of our having a simple pain in the reality, yet a delight in the representation, arises from hence, that we do not sufficiently distinguish what we would by no means choose to do, from what we should be eager enough to see if it was once done. The delight in seeing things, which, so far from doing, our heartiest wishes would be to see redressed. This noble capital, the pride of England and of Europe, I believe no man is so strangely wicked as to desire to see destroyed by a conflagration or an earthquake, though he should be removed himself to the greatest distance from the danger. But suppose such a fatal accident to have happened, what numbers from all parts would crowd to behold the ruins, and amongst many who would have been content never to have seen London in its glory! Nor is it, either in real or fictitious distresses, our immunity from them which produces our delight; in my own mind I can discover nothing like it. I apprehend that this mistake is owing to a sort of sophism, by which we are frequently imposed upon; it arises from our not distinguishing between what is indeed a necessary condition to our doing or suffering anything in general, and what is the cause of some particular act.

If a man kills me with a sword, it is a necessary condition to this that we should have been both of us alive before the fact; and yet it would be absurd to say, that our being both living creatures was the cause of his crime and of my death. So it is certain, that it is absolutely necessary my life should be out of any imminent hazard, before I can take a delight in the sufferings of others, real or imaginary, or indeed in anything else from any cause whatsoever. But then it is a sophism to argue from thence, that this immunity is the cause of my delight either on these or on any occasions. No one can distinguish such a cause of satisfaction in his own mind, I believe; nay, when we do not suffer any very acute pain, nor are exposed to any imminent danger of our lives, we can feel for others, whilst we suffer ourselves; and often then most when we are softened by affliction; we see with pity even distresses which we would accept in the place of our own.

On the Effects of Tragedy, Edmund Burke

Question 15:

According to the writer, why do we enjoy simulated tragedies?

A) Because they are not perfect.

B) Because we enjoy real calamities.

C) Because we know they are not real.

D) Because they please us.

Question 16:

According to the writer, what is the 'only difference' between a fictional movie of an earthquake and a real earthquake?

A) The real earthquake is a bigger calamity than a fictional earthquake.

B) The fictional earthquake is less convincing than a real earthquake.

C) The fictional earthquake has a lower death toll than a real earthquake.

D) We derive more pleasure from the fictional earthquake than from the real one.

Question 17:

In paragraph 1 what does the writer think is a 'mistake'?

A) To think that we don't gain pleasure from tragedy because it isn't real.

B) To think that the pleasure we get from tragedy is because it isn't real.

C) To think that the pleasure we get from tragedy is because it is close to reality.

D) To think that tragedy is a deceit because we enjoy it.

Question 18:

In paragraph 1, what principle would the writer most likely agree with?

A) Tragedy has the power to move us no matter if it is a fiction or real.

B) Tragedy is more powerful the closer it gets to fiction.

C) Tragedy is a deceit and its representations are not reality.

D) Tragedy becomes more powerful the closer it gets to reality.

Question 19:

Which statement would the writer most likely agree with?

A) People would choose to watch a real car crash than a fictional one.

B) People prefer to watch comedies rather than horrors.

C) People would prefer to see the perfect play about a murder than a real murder.

D) People enjoy seeing executions.

Question 20:

In paragraph 2, what principle would the writer most agree with?

A) We prefer to do evil things rather than just watch them.

B) We enjoy watching and participating in evil events.

C) We enjoy watching evil events that we would never choose to bring about.

D) We don't enjoy watching or bringing about evil events.

Question 21:

In paragraph 2, what does the writer mean by the word 'sophism'?

A) Error.

B) Understanding.

C) Fallacy.

D) Cause.

Question 22:

In paragraph 3, what does the writer think is 'absolutely necessary'?

A) Humans cannot enjoy tragedy if their lives are in danger.

B) Humans enjoy being in danger.

C) Humans can enjoy tragedies even if their lives are endangered.

D) Humans can take delight in the suffering of others

Question 23:

In the example given in paragraph 3, what does the writer think is 'absurd'?

A) Describing the cause of death as stabbing.

B) Describing the crime as being done by a living creature.

C) Describing 'being alive' as the cause of death.

D) Describing the necessary condition as being alive.

Question 24:

What is the writer's overall aim in writing this passage?

A) To discuss the genre of tragedy.

B) To explain why we enjoy tragedy.

C) To highlight how evil humankind is.

D) To explain the reasons for our different responses to real and fake tragedy.

Task Four

Read the text below, taken from a book by the Scottish philosopher David Hume.

It seems evident, that animals as well as men learn many things from experience, and infer, that the same events will always follow from the same causes. By this principle they become acquainted with the more obvious properties of external objects, and gradually, from their birth, treasure up a knowledge of the nature of fire, water, earth, stones, heights, depths, &c., and of the effects which result from their operation. The ignorance and inexperience of the young are here plainly distinguishable from the cunning and sagacity of the old, who have learned, by long observation, to avoid what hurt them, and to pursue what gave ease or pleasure. A horse, that has been accustomed to the field, becomes acquainted with the proper height which he can leap, and will never attempt what exceeds his force and ability. An old greyhound will trust the more fatiguing part of the chase to the younger, and will place himself so as to meet the hare in her doubles; nor are the conjectures, which he forms on this occasion, founded in any thing but his observation and experience.

This is still more evident from the effects of discipline and education on animals, who, by the proper application of rewards and punishments, may be taught any course of action, and most contrary to their natural instincts and propensities. Is it not experience, which renders a dog apprehensive of pain, when you menace him, or lift up the whip to beat him? Is it not even experience, which makes him answer to his name, and infer, from such an arbitrary sound, that you mean him rather than any of his fellows, and intend to call him, when you pronounce it in a certain manner, and with a certain tone and accent?

In all these cases, we may observe, that the animal infers some fact beyond what immediately strikes his senses; and that this inference is altogether founded on past experience, while the creature expects from the present object the same consequences, which it has always found in its observation to result from similar objects.

Of the Reason of Animals, David Hume

Question 25:
What does the writer claim about animals in paragraph 1?
A) Animals have a concept of cause and effect.
B) Animals are similar to humans in some respects.
C) Animals can reason.
D) All of the above.

Question 26:
What knowledge would an animal *not* be expected to have about the natural world, based on paragraph 1?
A) Water is wet.
B) The sky is sometimes blue.
C) A fall from a large height is painful.
D) Seven stones is a bigger quantity than six stones.

Question 27:
What does the writer say about old and young animals in paragraph 1?
A) Old animals are dull, and young animals are uneducated.
B) Old animals are deceitful, and young animals are inexperienced.
C) Old animals are devious, and young animals are stupid.
D) Old animals are wise and young animals are naïve.

Question 28:
Based on the examples in paragraph 1, what would the writer *not* agree with ?
A) An old rat learns to avoid cheese in mouse traps.
B) The young cat will miss-calculate the distance from the sofa to the table and will fall.
C) The young sled dog will pace himself at the beginning of a race.
D) An old horse will know that fire can burn down the barn.

Question 29:
What does the author *not* claim about disciplining animals in paragraph 2?

A) Animals can be taught to do anything.
B) Animals can be trained to act against their own deep instincts.
C) Animals can be educated.
D) Animals learn best through reward.

Question 30:
What is the writer's intentions in asking the questions in paragraph 2?
A) To rhetorically emphasise the correctness of his hypothesis.
B) To instil doubt about the importance of experience.
C) To lay out issues which he doesn't know the answer to.
D) To express puzzlement at aspects of dog behaviour.

Question 31:
In paragraph 2, the writer states 'this is still more evident…' What is still more evident?
A) The effects of discipline and punishment on animals.
B) The cunning of older animals compared to the inexperience of younger animals.
C) The fact that animals learn what hurts and helps them through experience.
D) That dogs learn through observation and experience.

Question 32:

Which example does not confirm the writer's theory in paragraph 3?

A) A dog learns that a ringing bell signals food, and he salivates when he hears the bell.

B) A dog associates a certain word with sitting, and so when he hears the word he sits down.

C) A dog is shouted at when he eats socks, and avoids socks in the future.

D) A dog sees a plate full of food, and he runs over to start eating.

Question 33:

What is the writer's main intention while writing this passage?

A) He intends this passage to be light-hearted and funny.

B) He intends this passage to be educational.

C) He intends this passage to be polemical.

D) He intends this passage to be reflective.

Question 34:

Which of the following animals does the writer refer to in this passage?

A) Horses, dogs, humans.

B) Humans, cats, horses, dogs, hares.

C) Humans, horses, hounds, dogs.

D) Hares, horses, dogs, humans.

Question 35:

What is the writer's main aim in this passage?

A) To emphasise the similarity between humans and animals.

B) To explain how animals learn and reason.

C) To describe the behaviour of horses and dogs.

D) To point out the importance of observation.

Question 36:

Based on this passage, overall, what would the writer most likely agree with?

A) Animals instinctually know what is dangerous and good for them.

B) Animals learn through experience.

C) Animals navigate the world mainly through innate knowledge.

D) Animals are incapable of reason.

Practice Paper A

Anglo Saxon, Norse, and Celtic

The passage below has been translated from Bede's *The Ecclesiastical History of the English People*, a major source for the history of late antiquity. There is no expectation that you will have seen it before, or be familiar with its context.

Read the passage and write an essay in response to one of the following:

How might a historian go about verifying detail contained in texts of this kind?

How might Bede's priorities as a historian have been different from those of historians today?

Chap. XIII. How in the reign of Theodosius the younger, in whose time Palladius was sent to the Scots that believed in Christ, the Britons begging assistance of Ætius, the consul, could not obtain it. [446 a.d.]

In the year of our Lord 423, Theodosius, the younger, the forty-fifth from Augustus, succeeded Honorius and governed the Roman empire twenty-six years. In the eighth year of his reign, 80 Palladius was sent by Celestinus, the Roman pontiff, to the Scots that believed in Christ, to be their first bishop. In the twenty-third year of his reign, Aetius, a man of note and a patrician, discharged his third consulship with Symmachus for his colleague. To him the wretched remnant of the Britons sent a letter, which began thus:—"To Aetius, thrice Consul, the groans of the Britons." And in the sequel of the letter they thus unfolded their woes:—"The barbarians drive us to the sea; the sea drives us back to the barbarians: between them we are exposed to two sorts of death; we are either slaughtered or drowned." Yet, for all this, they could not obtain any help from him, as he was then engaged in most serious wars with Bledla and Attila, kings of the Huns. And though the year before this Bledla had been murdered by the treachery of his own brother Attila, yet Attila himself remained so intolerable an enemy to the Republic, that he ravaged almost all Europe, attacking and destroying cities and castles. At the same time there was a famine at Constantinople, and soon after a plague followed; moreover, a great part of the wall of that city, with fifty-seven towers, fell to the ground. Many cities also went to ruin, and the famine and pestilential state of the air destroyed thousands of men and cattle.

Chap. XIV. How the Britons, compelled by the great famine, drove the barbarians out of their territories; and soon after there ensued, along with abundance of corn, decay of morals, pestilence, and the downfall of the nation.

In the meantime, the aforesaid famine distressing the Britons more and more, and leaving to posterity a lasting memory of its mischievous effects, obliged many of them to submit themselves to the depredators; though others still held out, putting their trust in God, when human help failed. These continually made raids from the mountains, caves, and woods, and, at length, began to inflict severe losses on their enemies, who had been for so many years plundering the country. The bold Irish robbers thereupon returned home, intending to come again before long. The Picts then settled down in the farthest part of the island and afterwards remained there, but they did not fail to plunder and harass the Britons from time to time.

Now, when the ravages of the enemy at length abated, the island began to abound with such plenty of grain as had never been known in any age before; along with plenty, evil living increased, and this was immediately attended by the taint of all manner of crime; in particular, cruelty, hatred of truth, and love of falsehood; insomuch, that if any one among them happened to be milder than the rest, and more inclined to truth, all the rest abhorred and persecuted him unrestrainedly, as if he had been the enemy of Britain. Nor were the laity only guilty of these things, but even our Lord's own flock, with its shepherds, casting off the easy yoke of Christ, gave themselves up to drunkenness, enmity, quarrels, strife, envy, and other such sins. In the meantime, on a sudden, a grievous plague fell upon that corrupt generation, which soon destroyed such numbers of them, that the living scarcely availed to bury the dead: yet, those that survived, could not be recalled from the spiritual death, which they had incurred through their sins, either by the death of their friends, or the fear of death. Whereupon, not long after, a more severe vengeance for their fearful crimes fell upon the sinful nation. They held a council to determine what was to be done, and where they should seek help to prevent or repel the cruel and frequent incursions of the northern nations; and in concert with their King Vortigern, it was unanimously decided to call the Saxons to their aid from beyond the sea, which, as the event plainly showed, was brought about by the Lord's will, that evil might fall upon them for their wicked deeds.

Asian and Middle Eastern Studies

The following passage in excerpted from Deng Xiaoping's famous speech of 1984, *Building Socialism with a Specifically Chinese Character.*, Read carefully and respond to the question below in English. You are not expected to recognise the text, but you should draw on your own knowledge of China and 20th century history in general in analysing the passage.

"When the People's Republic was founded, old China bequeathed us a broken economy with barely any industry. The economy was in chaos: there were food shortages and severe inflation. But we fed and employed the nation and stabilised commodity prices, and the economy quickly recovered. With this stable foundation we began to reconstruct. How did we do it? We relied on socialism and Marxism. Why did we choose socialism? We had to. Capitalism was a road to nowhere for China. If we had travelled down the capitalist road the chaos in China would never have ended, and we would never have wiped out poverty. This is why we are committed to adhering to the Marxist and socialist road. However, by "Marxism" we mean a Marxism that is combined with Chinese conditions, and by "socialism" we mean a socialism that is specially tailored to Chinese conditions with a distinctly Chinese character.

What do we mean by socialism and Marxism? In the past we were not so sure. Marxist theory emphasises the development of the productive forces. Socialism is the initial stage of communism, and at the advanced stage we will apply the principle "from each according to his ability, and to each according to his needs." This will require highly developed productive forces and an exceptional abundance of material wealth. Thus, the main task during the initial socialist stage is to develop the productive forces. The superiority of the socialist system compared to capitalism is proved by the faster and greater development of productive forces. As these forces develop, the people's lives will continually improve – both materially and culturally. After the People's Republic was founded, one of our failures was that we did not attend enough to developing the productive forces. Socialism is about eradicating poverty. Poverty is not socialist nor communist.

The current world is open. The main reason China was so backward after the Western industrial revolution was because of its closed-door policy. When the People's Republic was founded, other countries blockaded us so the country remained closed – this created huge problems for us. The past thirty years has made clear to us that a closed-door policy would hinder development."

What distinctions does Deng draw in this speech?

What are the implications for China's position relative to the rest of the world?

What does government with Chinese characteristics mean today?

Education

Read the following passage and answer one question only.

It's summer time, and I have a proposal to parents who want to gift their kids the magic of reading: grab Siegfried Engelmann's *Teach Your Child to Read in 100 Easy Lessons*. I used this book with my then-four-year-old chid, and after just 20 minutes a night my little girl (who at the start of summer could only read the words 'no' and 'stop', and her own name) could, by autumn, read easy books by herself.

Engelmanns' book, which he co-wrote with Phyllis Haddox and Elaine Bruner, was initially published in the 1980s, and it was based on research from the late 1960s. In the 60s Engelmann was involved in a government project called 'Follow Through', which compared nine different methods for how to teach children reading. The project tracked 75,000 children from nursery through to third grade of school. The results were clear (although some skeptics have criticised them on methodological grounds): the best way to teach children to read was based on phonics. The phonics system involves teaching children how to sound words out letter by letter, rather than learning whole words at a time. The most successful method built on basic phonics with a learning format that emphasised repetition and student participation: this is called the 'direct instruction' method. The results were equally impressive for poor children, including black ones.

But in the education world today, Engelmann's technique is controversial..."

How I Taught my Kid to Read, John McWhorter

Why might Engelmann's technique be considered controversial?

How does the direct instruction method described in the passage contrast with your own understanding of learning to read?

Why might teachers be resistant to the direct instruction method?

What does this approach to learning suggest about how children learn?

History

Compare and contrast the characterisations of institution of monarchy offered in these two passages.

Mankind being originally equals in the order of creation, the equality could only be destroyed by some subsequent circumstance; the distinctions of rich, and poor, may in a great measure be accounted for, and that without having recourse to the harsh ill sounding names of oppression and avarice. Oppression is often the consequence, but seldom or never the means of riches; and though avarice will preserve a man from being necessitously poor, it generally makes him too timorous to be wealthy.

But there is another and greater distinction for which no truly natural or religious reason can be assigned, and that is, the distinction of men into kings and subjects. Male and female are the distinctions of nature, good and bad the distinctions of heaven; but how a race of men came into the world so exalted above the rest, and distinguished like some new species, is worth enquiring into, and whether they are the means of happiness or of misery to mankind.

In the early ages of the world, according to the scripture chronology, there were no kings; the consequence of which was there were no wars; it is the pride of kings which throw mankind into confusion. Holland without a king hath enjoyed more peace for this last century than any of the monarchial governments in Europe. Antiquity favors the same remark; for the quiet and rural lives of the first patriarchs hath a happy something in them, which vanishes away when we come to the history of Jewish royalty.

Government by kings was first introduced into the world by the Heathens, from whom the children of Israel copied the custom. It was the most prosperous invention the Devil ever set on foot for the promotion of idolatry. The Heathens paid divine honors to their deceased kings, and the christian world hath improved on the plan by doing the same to their living ones. How impious is the title of sacred majesty applied to a worm, who in the midst of his splendor is crumbling into dust!

As the exalting one man so greatly above the rest cannot be justified on the equal rights of nature, so neither can it be defended on the authority of scripture; for the will of the Almighty, as declared by Gideon and the prophet Samuel, expressly disapproves of government by kings. All anti-monarchical parts of scripture have been very smoothly glossed over in monarchical governments, but they undoubtedly merit the attention of countries which have their governments yet to form. "Render unto Cæsar the things which are Cæsar's" is the scripture doctrine of courts, yet it is no support of monarchical government, for the Jews at that time were without a king, and in a state of vassalage to the Romans.

Common Sense, Thomas Paine

These new Whigs hold that the sovereignty, whether exercised by one or many, did not only originate from the people, (a position not denied nor worth denying or assenting to,) but that in the people the same sovereignty constantly and unalienably resides; that the people may lawfully depose kings, not only for misconduct, but without any misconduct at all; that they may set up any new fashion of government for themselves, or continue without any government, at their pleasure; that the people are essentially their own rule, and their will the measure of their conduct; that the tenure of magistracy is not a proper subject of contract, because magistrates have duties, but no rights; and that, if a contract de facto is made with them in one age, allowing that it binds at all, it only binds those who are immediately concerned in it, but does not pass to posterity. These doctrines concerning the people (a term which they are far from accurately defining, but by which, from many circumstances, it is plain enough they mean their own faction, if they should grow, by early arming, by treachery, or violence, into the prevailing force) tend, in my opinion, to the utter subversion, not only of all government, in all modes, and to all stable securities to rational freedom, but to all the rules and principles of morality itself

An Appeal from the Old Whigs to the New, Edmund Burke

Human, Social, and Political Sciences

Choose one of the questions below only.

Assessment of your answer will take into account the overall coherence and persuasiveness of your argument, your ability to use relevant evidence to support it, and the clarity and quality of your English.

Is American politics democratic?

Should women have their own representatives?

Practice Paper B

Anglo Saxon, Norse, and Celtic

The passage below has been translated from Geoffrey of Monmouth's *The History of the Kings of Britain*, a work of pseudohistory written in the 12th Century. There is no expectation that you will have seen it before, or be familiar with its context.

Read the passage and write an essay in response to one of the following questions:

Did Monmouth believe that he was recording facts in this passage? If not, why not?

What does the interweaving of factual and fictional characters suggest about pre modern history writing?

As Vortigern, king of the Britons, was sitting upon the bank of the drained pond, the two dragons, one of which was white, the other red, came forth, and, approaching one another, began a terrible fight, and cast forth fire with their breath. But the white dragon had the advantage, and made the other fly to the end of the lake. And he, for grief at his flight, renewed the assault upon his pursuer, and forced him to retire. After this battle of the dragons, the king commanded Ambrose Merlin to tell him what it portended. Upon which he, bursting into tears, delivered what his prophetical spirit suggested to him, as follows:—

"Woe to the red dragon, for his banishment hasteneth on. His lurking holes shall be seized by the white dragon, which signifies the Saxons whom you invited over; but the red denotes the British nation, which shall be oppressed by the white. Therefore shall its mountains be levelled as the valleys, and the rivers of the valleys shall run with blood. The exercise of religion shall be destroyed, and churches laid open to ruin. At last the oppressed shall prevail, and oppose the cruelty of foreigners. For a boar of Cornwall shall give his assistance, and trample their necks under his feet. The islands of the ocean shall be subject to his power, and he shall possess the forests of Gaul. The house of Romulus shall dread his courage, and his end shall be doubtful. He shall be celebrated in the mouths of the people; and his exploits shall be food to those that relate them. Six of his posterity shall sway the sceptre, but after them shall arise a German worm. He shall be advanced by a sea-wolf, whom the woods of Africa shall accompany. Religion shall again be abolished, and there shall be a translation of the metropolitan sees. The dignity of London shall adorn Dorobernia, and the seventh pastor of York shall be resorted to in the kingdom of Armorica. St David's shall put on the pall of the City of Legions, and a preacher of Ireland shall be dumb on account of an infant growing in the womb. It shall rain a shower of blood, and a raging famine shall afflict mankind. When these things happen, the red one shall be grieved; but when his fatigue is over, shall grow strong. Then shall misfortunes hasten upon the white one, and the buildings of his gardens shall be pulled down. Seven that sway the sceptre shall be killed, one of whom shall become a saint. The wombs of mothers shall be ripped up, and infants be abortive. There shall be a most grievous punishment of men, that the natives may be restored. He that shall do these things shall put on the brazen man, and upon a brazen horse shall for a long time guard the gates of London. After this, shall the red dragon return to his proper manners, and turn his rage upon himself. Therefore shall the revenge of the Thunderer show itself, for every field shall disappoint the husbandmen. Mortality shall snatch away the people, and make a desolation over all countries. The remainder shall quit their native soil, and make foreign plantations. A blessed king shall prepare a fleet, and shall be reckoned the twelfth in the court among the saints. There shall be a miserable desolation of the kingdom, and the floors of the harvests shall return to the fruitful forests. The white dragon shall rise again, and invite over a daughter of Germany. Our gardens shall be again replenished with foreign seed, and the red one shall pine away at the end of the pond.

Asian and Middle Eastern Studies

The following passage is excerpted from the classic Chinese novel *Romance of the Three Kingdoms*. Read carefully and respond to the question below in English. You are not expected to recognise the text, and no credit will be given for referring to other parts of the novel.

Let us now turn to Sun Jian's sons, four of whom were the offspring of Lady Wu. The given name of the oldest was Ce, whose style name was Bofu; the given name of his second son was Quan, whose style name was Zhongmou; the given name of his third son was Yi, whose style name was Shubi; the given name of his fourth son was Kuang, whose style name was Jizuo; Lady Wu's younger sister was Sun Jian's second wife. She also bore him one son and one daughter. The given name of the son was Lang, whose style name was Zao'an; the daughter's given name was Ren. Jian had also adopted a boy from the Yu family, whose given name was Shao, and whose style name was Gongli. Jian had one younger brother, whose given name was Jing, and whose style name was Youtai.

Just prior to Jian's departure, Jing brought forward all of Jian's sons and had them pay obeisance by order of age in front of Jian's horse. Jing then admonished Jian, saying, "Dong Zhuo is now monopolizing all power, and the Son of Heaven is cowardly and weak. The nation is in chaos, and everyone has made a grab for their own turf. The eastern bank of the Yangtze has only recently been pacified. Raising such a massive army over a minor slight wouldn't be prudent. Older brother, I hope that you take that into consideration." Jian said, "Younger brother, you will say no more. I must have license to do as I please anywhere in the country; in light of that, how can I not avenge a slight?" Sun Ce, Jian's oldest son, said, "Father, if you must go, I will accompany you. After all, I am your son." Jian gave his consent, and then boarded the war junk, along with Ce. Together, they set their sights on attacking Fancheng.

Huang Zu hid his archers on the river bank; when they saw the boats approaching the shore, they let loose with a wild flurry of arrows. Jian ordered his troops to take no rash actions, but rather to hide in the hold of the boats. The boats were to advance and withdraw in order to bait the enemy into firing. Over the course of three days, they approached the shore dozens of times. Huang Zu's army thought of nothing else but shooting their arrows; eventually, they exhausted their supply. Jian ordered his men to fish the hundreds of thousands of arrows out of the water. The winds were favorable on that day; Jian ordered his troops to shoot the arrows in unison. The forces on shore could not hold their ground, and had no choice but to withdraw.

What do we learn about Chinese family culture from this passage?

What general principles are suggested by Jian's stratagem?

Education

Read the following passage and answer one question only.

Imagine that a law firm wants to hire a summer associate. A law student with a PhD in philosophy from Berkeley applies. What do you infer about this candidate? The candidate is probably dedicated, brilliant, and willing to put up with seriously boring work. If you want to hire that kind of employee – and most employers do – you will give them an offer, even though you know that nothing they learned while studying philosophy at Berkeley will be relevant to the law job.

The labour market doesn't hire and pay you for your mastery of the useless subjects you have studied: it pays you for the character traits and skills you exhibit by mastering them. This is not a niche idea. Multiple Nobel laureates in economics, such as Spence, Arrow, and Stiglitz, all contributed to the theory of 'educational signalling'. And every single university student who does the least amount of work to get good grades implicitly endorses this theory. Yet educational signalling is nowhere to be found in government policy or public discourse. Our society continues to encourage ever increasing numbers of students into even higher levels of education. The main outcome is not greater skill levels or better jobs, but a credentials arms race.

At the risk of being misunderstood, I emphatically state that education does confer some marketable skills. Students become literate and numerate. However, I do believe that educational signalling constitutes at least half of university's financial reward – and maybe even more.

The main salary payoff for university is derived from crossing the finishing line at graduation. Imagine a student who drops out after one year. She will gain a salary increase compared with a person who has not attended any university, but it won't be anywhere near as high as the 25 percent salary bonus she would get if she completed a four-year degree. Similarly, the salary bonus for completing second year is nowhere near the 50% of the return on a degree. Indeed, studies show that the final year of college brings more than twice the pay increase of first year, second year, and third year combined. Universities are not delaying job training until the very end of the course, and so signalling is the best explanation for what is going on here. This implies that a huge number of resources are being wasted. Students' money and time would be better spent preparing them for the jobs they are likely to be hired to do in the future.

The Case Against Education, Bryan Caplan

Why might Caplan's views be considered controversial?

How much of the value of education do you think is signalling?

Defend the conventional model of college education from Caplan's attack

If you could never tell anyone you attended Cambridge, or put it on your CV, would you still have applied?

History

Compare and contrast the rights and responsibilities outlined in these two passages.

Article I – Men are born and remain free and equal in rights. Social distinctions can be founded only on the common good.

Article II – The goal of any political association is the conservation of the natural and imprescriptible rights of man. These rights are liberty, property, safety and resistance against oppression.

Article III – The principle of any sovereignty resides essentially in the Nation. No body, no individual may exercise any authority which does not proceed directly from the nation

Article IV – Liberty consists of doing anything which does not harm others: thus, the exercise of the natural rights of each man has only those borders which assure other members of the society the fruition of these same rights. These borders can be determined only by the law.

Article V – The law has the right to forbid only actions harmful to society. Anything which is not forbidden by the law cannot be impeded, and no one can be constrained to do what it does not order.

Article VI – The law is the expression of the general will. All the citizens have the right of contributing personally or through their representatives to its formation. It must be the same for all, either that it protects, or that it punishes. All the citizens, being equal in its eyes, are equally admissible to all public dignities, places, and employments, according to their capacity and without distinction other than that of their virtues and of their talents.

Article VII – No man can be accused, arrested nor detained but in the cases determined by the law, and according to the forms which it has prescribed. Those who solicit, dispatch, carry out or cause to be carried out arbitrary orders, must be punished; but any citizen called or seized under the terms of the law must obey at once; he renders himself culpable by resistance.

Article VIII – The law should establish only penalties that are strictly and evidently necessary, and no one can be punished but under a law established and promulgated before the offense and legally applied.

Article IX – Any man being presumed innocent until he is declared culpable if it is judged indispensable to arrest him, any rigor which would not be necessary for the securing of his person must be severely reprimanded by the law.

Article X – No one may be disturbed for his opinions, even religious ones, provided that their manifestation does not trouble the public order established by the law.

Article XI – The free communication of thoughts and of opinions is one of the most precious rights of man: any citizen thus may speak, write, print freely, except to respond to the abuse of this liberty, in the cases determined by the law.

Article XII – The guarantee of the rights of man and of the citizen necessitates a public force: this force is thus instituted for the advantage of all and not for the particular utility of those in whom it is trusted.

Article XIII – For the maintenance of the public force and for the expenditures of administration, a common contribution is indispensable; it must be equally distributed to all the citizens, according to their ability to pay.

Article XIV – Each citizen has the right to ascertain, by himself or through his representatives, the need for a public tax, to consent to it freely, to know the uses to which it is put, and of determining the proportion, basis, collection, and duration.

Article XV – The society has the right of requesting an account from any public agent of its administration.

Article XVI – Any society in which the guarantee of rights is not assured, nor the separation of powers determined, has no Constitution.

Article XVII – Property being an inviolable and sacred right, no one can be deprived of private usage, if it is not when the public necessity, legally noted, evidently requires it, and under the condition of a just and prior indemnity.

Declaration of Rights of Man and Citizen, Sieyes and Lafayette, 1789

Article 1

All human beings are born free and equal in dignity and rights. They are endowed with reason and conscience and should act towards one another in a spirit of brotherhood.

Article 2

Everyone is entitled to all the rights and freedoms set forth in this Declaration, without distinction of any kind, such as race, colour, sex, language, religion, political or other opinion, national or social origin, property, birth or other status.

Furthermore, no distinction shall be made on the basis of the political, jurisdictional or international status of the country or territory to which a person belongs, whether it be independent, trust, non-self-governing or under any other limitation of sovereignty.

Article 3

Everyone has the right to life, liberty and the security of person.

Article 4

No one shall be held in slavery or servitude; slavery and the slave trade shall be prohibited in all their forms.

Article 5

No one shall be subjected to torture or to cruel, inhuman or degrading treatment or punishment.

Article 6

Everyone has the right to recognition everywhere as a person before the law.

Article 7

All are equal before the law and are entitled without any discrimination to equal protection of the law. All are entitled to equal protection against any discrimination in violation of this Declaration and against any incitement to such discrimination.

Article 8

Everyone has the right to an effective remedy by the competent national tribunals for acts violating the fundamental rights granted him by the constitution or by law.

Article 9

No one shall be subjected to arbitrary arrest, detention or exile.

Article 10

Everyone is entitled in full equality to a fair and public hearing by an independent and impartial tribunal, in the determination of his rights and obligations and of any criminal charge against him.

Article 11

1. Everyone charged with a penal offence has the right to be presumed innocent until proved guilty according to law in a public trial at which he has had all the guarantees necessary for his defence.

2. No one shall be held guilty of any penal offence on account of any act or omission which did not constitute a penal offence, under national or international law, at the time when it was committed. Nor shall a heavier penalty be imposed than the one that was applicable at the time the penal offence was committed.

Article 12

No one shall be subjected to arbitrary interference with his privacy, family, home or correspondence, nor to attacks upon his honour and reputation. Everyone has the right to the protection of the law against such interference or attacks.

United Nations Universal Declaration of Human Rights, 1948

Human, Social, and Political Sciences

Choose one of the questions below only.

Assessment of your answer will take into account the overall coherence and persuasiveness of your argument, your ability to use relevant evidence to support it, and the clarity and quality of your English.

Are there conditions under which the outcomes of democratic election should be ignored?

If you could interview a relative who lived through World War II, what would you expect to learn about the main ways society has changed since the war, and what might make their perspective distinct?

Practice Paper C

Anglo Saxon, Norse, and Celtic

The passage below has been translated from Beowulf. There is no expectation that you will have seen it before or be familiar with its context. You will not receive additional credit for referring to other passages of the poem than the one provided.

Read the passage and write an essay in response to one of the following questions:

What choices has the translator made in this version of the text? Why do you think he has made them?

The authorship of Beowulf is unknown. What challenges might this pose for a literature student studying the poem? And for a historian? Are these challenges different?

Lo, praise of the prowess of people-kings
of spear-armed Danes, in days long sped,
we have heard, and what honor the athelings won!
Oft Scyld the Scefing from squadroned foes,
5from many a tribe, the mead-bench tore,
awing the earls. Since erst he lay
friendless, a foundling, fate repaid him:
for he waxed under welkin, in wealth he throve,
till before him the folk, both far and near,
who house by the whale-path, heard his mandate,
gave him gifts: a good king he!
To him an heir was afterward born,
a son in his halls, whom heaven sent
to favor the folk, feeling their woe
that erst they had lacked an earl for leader
so long a while; the Lord endowed him,
the Wielder of Wonder, with world's renown.
Famed was this Beowulf: far flew the boast of him,
son of Scyld, in the Scandian lands.
So becomes it a youth to quit him well
with his father's friends, by fee and gift,
that to aid him, agéd, in after days,
come warriors willing, should war draw nigh,
liegemen loyal: by lauded deeds
shall an earl have honor in every clan.
Forth he fared at the fated moment,
sturdy Scyld to the shelter of God.
Then they bore him over to ocean's billow,
loving clansmen, as late he charged them,
while wielded words the winsome Scyld,
the leader belovéd who long had ruled. . . .
In the roadstead rocked a ring-dight vessel,
ice-flecked, outbound, atheling's barge:
there laid they down their darling lord
on the breast of the boat, the breaker-of-rings,

by the mast the mighty one. Many a treasure
fetched from far was freighted with him.
No ship have I known so nobly dight
with weapons of war and weeds of battle,
with breastplate and blade: on his bosom lay
a heapéd hoard that hence should go
far o'er the flood with him floating away.
No less these loaded the lordly gifts,
thanes' huge treasure, than those had done
who in former time forth had sent him
sole on the seas, a suckling child.
High o'er his head they hoist the standard,
a gold-wove banner; let billows take him,
gave him to ocean. Grave were their spirits,
mournful their mood. No man is able
to say in sooth, no son of the halls,
no hero 'neath heaven,—who harbored that freight!

Asian and Middle Eastern Studies

Read the following passage, excerpted from an April 1997 issue of *The Economist* magazine, and respond to the essay question below.

Many westerners regard the handover of Hong Kong to China as a travesty and a tragedy. For the first time, Britain handed a colony directly to a Communist regime that does not respect democratic values. If China responds to Hong Kong with an armoured fist a real tragedy might actually occur. But if China's hand is gentle, and it fulfils its promise to let Hong Kong preserve its own way of life, much of what makes this territory special should endure.

There is another intriguing possibility. What if China didn't take over Hong Kong, but Hong Kong took over China? Preposterous? Not necessarily. Something like this is already happening, economically. In 1978 China abandoned the policy of self-sufficient socialism. Since then, the Chinese economy has been transferred by foreign investment 60% of which derives from Hong Kong. Money and expertise from Hong Kong triggered a booming manufacturing industry in South China, and Hong Kong cash is rebuilding China's business capital city, Shanghai. In the last 20 years, it is fair to say that China's economy has become more like Hong Kong's than vice versa.

The economy is one thing, but is it plausible that something similar could happen with regards to the rule of law and politics? The Chinese Communist leaders are strongly against this idea. According to them, Hong Kong is an 'economic' city. In fact, the one condition that China insists on when it promise to preserve Hong Kong's way of life is that it must never become base for "subversion" on the mainland. When the Chinese government takes over, their first action will be to swear in a Beijing- appointed legislature to replace the democratically elected one. Worries about the independence of the judiciary and press freedom in Hong Kong are well founded.

But the introspective members of Beijing's political class must be aware that China's centralised system of governmental control is savage, inefficient, and innately unstable. If used thoughtfully and carefully Hong Kong could serve as a kind of laboratory for political changes in China. China is finding it difficult to establish a credible legal justice system to accompany its economy; Hong Kong already has a reliable legal system. China will flaunt its experiments with 'village democracy', but claims that universal democracy requires a more developed, sophisticated, and wealthier society; Hong Kong is such a society. And despite the dismantling of the elected legislature in Hong Kong, China has promised elections within the year. In all likelihood these elections will be tampered with to ensure that nobody disagreeable to the Beijing authorities gains any power.

The braver and more rational decision would be to allow a real election, so that a part of China could experiment with a more democratic and modern political system."

What lessons about the nature of colonialism might be drawn from the experience of Hong Kong?

How have Western views of the handover changed since 1997?

Education

Read the following abstract and answer one question only.

In many developing nations, private tutoring is a major part of the education sector. However, government education policies very seldom acknowledge and make use of private tutoring. Critics of tutoring argue that it fails to improve student outcomes and deepens social inequalities. In this paper, I examine the evidence on private tutoring. I analyse the extent of tutoring, how cost effective it is, and reasons that explain its growth. I also assess the efficiency and equity effects of tutoring. I conclude that tutoring can, under certain assumptions, increase the effectiveness of the overall education system – even when equity concerns are taken into account. I offer practical advice for countering corruption and other issues that diminish the efficacy of the private tutoring sector.

How to Interpret the Growing Phenomenon of Private Tutoring: Human Capital Deepening, Inequality Increasing, or Waste of Resources?, World Bank Working Paper, 2008

How might the value of private tuition differ between developed and developing economies?

How important do you see education in combating inequality

Should education aim to reduce inequality directly, or only through indirect mechanisms?

Do you think private tuition for university applications is fair? If not, how might universities go about ensuring it doesn't unfairly advantage applicants?

History

The passage below is the first article of the Treaty of Tordesillas, in which Spain and Portugal divided up the New World between them at the end of the 15th Century. Write a short essay on its implications and consequences.

That, whereas a certain controversy exists between the said lords, their constituents, as to what lands, of all those discovered in the ocean sea up to the present day, the date of this treaty, pertain to each one of the said parts respectively; therefore, for the sake of peace and concord, and for the preservation of the relationship and love of the said King of Portugal for the said King and Queen of Castile, Aragon, etc., it being the pleasure of their Highnesses, they, their said representatives, acting in their name and by virtue of their powers herein described, covenanted and agreed that a boundary or straight line be determined and drawn north and south, from pole to pole, on the said ocean sea, from the Arctic to the Antarctic pole.

This boundary or line shall be drawn straight, as aforesaid, at a distance of three hundred and seventy leagues west of the Cape Verde Islands, being calculated by degrees, or by any other manner as may be considered the best and readiest, provided the distance shall be no greater than abovesaid. And all lands, both islands and mainlands, found and discovered already, or to be found and discovered hereafter, by the said King of Portugal and by his vessels on this side of the said line and bound determined as above, toward the east, in either north or south latitude, on the eastern side of the said bound provided the said bound is not crossed, shall belong to, and remain in the possession of, and pertain forever to, the said King of Portugal and his successors.

And all other lands, both islands and mainlands, found or to be found hereafter, discovered or to be discovered hereafter, which have been discovered or shall be discovered by the said King and Queen of Castile, Aragon, etc., and by their vessels, on the western side of the said bound, determined as above, after having passed the said bound toward the west, in either its north or south latitude, shall belong to, and remain in the possession of, and pertain forever to, the said King and Queen of Castile, Leon, etc., and to their successors.

Treaty of Tordesillas, 1494

Human, Social, and Political Sciences

Choose one of the questions below only.

Assessment of your answer will take into account the overall coherence and persuasiveness of your argument, your ability to use relevant evidence to support it, and the clarity and quality of your English.

Does the recent migration crisis in Europe challenge or reinforce racism?

What embarrasses people and what does embarrassment reveal about how they regard themselves?

Practice Paper D

Anglo Saxon, Norse, and Celtic

The passage below has been translated from *The Kalevala*, a 19th Century verse reconstruction of ancient Finnish folklore. There is no expectation that you will have seen it before or be familiar with its context.

Read the passage and write an essay in response to one of the following questions.

Why might an author decide to attempt a project such as this?

What might they prioritise this kind of work?

What can we learn about Finnish identity from a work like this?

What does it mean for a modern author to write a consciously old fashioned work such as this?

WAINAMOINEN, thus encouraged,
Quickly rises in his snow-sledge,
Asking no one for assistance,
Straightway hastens to the cottage,
Takes a seat within the dwelling.
Come two maids with silver pitchers,
Bringing also golden goblets;
Dip they up a very little,
But the very smallest measure
Of the blood of the magician,
From the wounds of Wainamoinen.
From the fire-place calls the old man,
Thus the gray-beard asks the minstrel:
"Tell me who thou art of heroes,
Who of all the great magicians?
Lo! thy blood fills seven sea-boats,
Eight of largest birchen vessels,
Flowing from some hero's veinlets,
From the wounds of some magician.
Other matters I would ask thee;
Sing the cause of this thy trouble,
Sing to me the source of metals,
Sing the origin of iron,
How at first it was created."
Then the ancient Wainamoinen
Made this answer to the gray-beard:
"Know I well the source of metals,
Know the origin of iron;
f can tell bow steel is fashioned.
Of the mothers air is oldest,
Water is the oldest brother,
And the fire is second brother,
And the youngest brother, iron;

Ukko is the first creator.
Ukko, maker of the heavens,
Cut apart the air and water,
Ere was born the metal, iron.
Ukko, maker of the heavens,
Firmly rubbed his hands together,
Firmly pressed them on his knee-cap,
Then arose three lovely maidens,
Three most beautiful of daughters;
These were mothers of the iron,
And of steel of bright-blue color.
Tremblingly they walked the heavens,
Walked the clouds with silver linings,
With their bosoms overflowing
With the milk of future iron,
Flowing on and flowing ever,
From the bright rims of the cloudlets
To the earth, the valleys filling,
To the slumber-calling waters.

Asian and Middle Eastern Studies

Read the passage of journalistic writing which summarises some ethnographic work below and respond to the essay question.

In the 1540s, a Portuguese missionary and merchant called António de Paiva arrived at Sulawesi in Indonesia. His goal was to set up trade with the local Bugis people, and convert them to Christianity, while fending off conversion attempts from Muslim missionaries. De Paiva believed his task would be simple: pork was a staple of the local diet, and he thought this would be enough to persuade the local rulers to choose Christianity instead of Islam (which forbids the consumption of pork.) What he didn't count on was the influence of the bissu.

In a letter written in 1544 to the Portuguese bishop of Goa, João de Albuquerque, De Paiva wrote:

Your Lordship will know that the priests of these kings are generally called bissus. They grow no hair on their beards, dress in a womanly fashion, and grow their hair long and braided; they imitate [women's] speech because they adopt all of the female gestures and inclinations. They marry and are received, according to the custom of the land, with other common men, and they live indoors, uniting carnally in their secret places with the men whom they have for husbands ... These priests, if they touch a woman in thought or deed, are boiled in tar because they hold that all their religion would be lost if they did it; and they have their teeth covered in gold. Unluckily for De Paiva, the bissu wielded enormous power over their rulers, and they convinced them to convert to Islam. To this day we don't really know why the bissu preferred Islam, but it is clear that their influence was considerable.

The bissu are still powerful. They are a group of spiritual leaders (akin to a shaman or a priest) who perform all kinds of tasks for the community, such as advising on marriage, debt settlements, and optimal crop harvest dates. Nowadays, long after their conversion to Islam, they bless those about to embark on the Islamic pilgrimage to Mecca. Where does this power and influence come from?

The Bugis people believe that when a being became a man or a woman, the being could no longer communicate with the gods. Men and women became isolated from the gods that created them. But the bissu were chosen humans who could communicate with the gods. The gods made the bissu a combination of man and woman, and so they are granted a position of influence. The bissu are man and woman combined in one person, and so can mediate between the gods and humans via blessings. "

How does the Bugis understanding of gender contrast with De Paiva's?

And with our contemporary Western ideas?

What ideas are at stake in religious conversion?

Education

In order to understand Steiner/Waldorf education, one must go back to the Germany of 1919, which was socially ruined after World War 1. Intellectuals despaired at the depth of social inequality, made worse by national defeat. This was a time open to radical new ideas. These conditions enabled Rudolf Steiner to postulate a new social order, founded upon a radical interpretation of the time-honoured concepts of liberty, equality, and fraternity.

Fundamental to this was the separation of the three spheres of culture (freedom), rights (equality), and economics (fraternity), a principle known as 'social threefolding'. Steiner's whole philosophy revolved around freedom. Education is in the sphere of culture, and it is essential that school should serve children and not the state. The ultimate aim of Steiner/Waldorf schools is to cultivate fully free human beings, but they operate on the assumption that freedom is not granted just by virtue of an arbitrary declaration of human rights. For these schools, freedom is not a method of education. It is, rather, a consequence of it.

Education for Freedom, Ashley Martin

How do you understand the relationship between the state and schooling?

Are private schools fundamentally different from state schools?

Should education be centred on freedom as a goal, or focus on specific educational and social outcomes?

Are the ideals of the Steiner movement achievable at scale? If not, why?

History

[handwritten: generalistic tone]   *[handwritten: - persuasive text - emphasises the attainable]*

The passages below, from John F Kennedy's address to American University, widely known as The Peace Speech, and Malenkov's "Peace Offensive" speech. Write a short essay contrasting the two speeches and exploring their implications and consequences.

Let us examine our attitude toward peace itself. Too many of us think it is impossible. Too many think it unreal. But that is a dangerous, defeatist belief. It leads to the conclusion that war is inevitable--that mankind is doomed--that we are gripped by forces we cannot control.

We need not accept that view. Our problems are manmade--therefore, they can be solved by man. And man can be as big as he wants. No problem of human destiny is beyond human beings. Man's reason and spirit have often solved the seemingly unsolvable--and we believe they can do it again.

I am not referring to the absolute, infinite concept of peace and good will of which some fantasies and fanatics dream. I do not deny the value of hopes and dreams but we merely invite discouragement and incredulity by making that our only and immediate goal.

Let us focus instead on a more practical, more attainable peace-- based not on a sudden revolution in human nature but on a gradual evolution in human institutions--on a series of concrete actions and effective agreements which are in the interest of all concerned. There is no single, simple key to this peace--no grand or magic formula to be adopted by one or two powers. Genuine peace must be the product of many nations, the sum of many acts. It must be dynamic, not static, changing to meet the challenge of each new generation. For peace is a process--a way of solving problems.

With such a peace, there will still be quarrels and conflicting interests, as there are within families and nations. World peace, like community peace, does not require that each man love his neighbor--it requires only that they live together in mutual tolerance, submitting their disputes to a just and peaceful settlement. And history teaches us that enmities between nations, as between individuals, do not last forever. However fixed our likes and dislikes may seem, the tide of time and events will often bring surprising changes in the relations between nations and neighbors.

So let us persevere. Peace need not be impracticable, and war need not be inevitable. By defining our goal more clearly, by making it seem more manageable and less remote, we can help all peoples to see it, to draw hope from it, and to move irresistibly toward it.

John F Kennedy, 1963

[handwritten: informative]

[handwritten: How to obtain peace]

[handwritten: Changing Nature of peace]

[handwritten: contemporary.]

[handwritten: Evolution of Humans - varies the extent to which peace can be achieved]

[handwritten: What is peace?]

In the international sphere the Soviet Union, in close co-operation with the Chinese People's Republic, with all the people's democracies, has scored big successes in the lofty cause of upholding and strengthening peace.

The Soviet Union's consistently pursued policy of developing contacts and peaceful relations with all states is a salient feature of the past years. All peoples see the Soviet Union's energetic efforts to strengthen peace throughout the world. The U.S.S.R. has graphically and convincingly demonstrated that in its entire foreign policy it adheres strictly to the Leninist principle of peaceful co-existence of countries with different social systems. The peace initiative and steadfast peace policy of the Soviet Union have considerably strengthened the positions of the U.S.S.R. and the entire socialist camp in the international arena.

In the domestic sphere the past period is characterised by a fresh upsurge of the national economy and a rise in the living standards of the Soviet people. The immense work accomplished by the Communist Party has resulted in an enhancement of the might of our socialist state, further con-solidation of the moral and political unity of Soviet society and the fraternal friendship of the peoples of the Soviet Union, and in the strengthening of Soviet law and socialist democracy.

In the report of the central committee, N. S. Khrushchov noted with full justification that during the period under review the political leadership of the party's central committee has been at an adequate level and that the party has worked out correct solutions to problems connected with the development of the state and the party, and has competently led the country along the Leninist path.

The general results of the country's development since the 19th Congress of the party show that the rate of growth of the Soviet Union's economy remains at a level unknown to the capitalist countries. The advance of its national economy continues and is based on the implementation of a programme for peaceful construction.

Georgy Malenkov, 1955

[handwritten annotations:] Peace is presented as a revolutionary achievement.

Economic upsurge.

What is the purpose
- Embellish the strengths of a socialist regime

Human, Social, and Political Sciences

Choose one of the questions below only.

Assessment of your answer will take into account the overall coherence and persuasiveness of your argument, your ability to use relevant evidence to support it, and the clarity and quality of your English.

Must all revolutions necessarily fail?

What are the major causes (and consequences) of global inequality?

Specimen Paper

Task One

Question 1: B

The author writes that ICT and e-participation shapes democratic reform. The overall gist is that e-democracy will be a catalyst for democratic reform. It's not A, because e-democracy is said to work alongside traditional forms of democracy (so is not preferable). It's not C, because the future is not discussed in this article. It's not D because other approaches are not discussed.

Question 2: B

The goal of active civic engagement is contrasted with the current functions of e-government applications, which are 'one way'. It's not D because 'two way ongoing dialogue' is part of active civic engagements so is not a contrast. It's not C, because the contrast is not between e-government and e-democracy per se but their goals. It's not A because greater civic participation is practically synonymous with active civic engagement.

Question 3: A

The authors reduce the theories into four idealised models and say that all the current theories of e-democracy may be covered by them. These models are enough for a complete analysis of e-democracy.

Question 4: B

The authors say that the four models are 'idealised' which suggests they don't full represent reality, but are stylised models of how various systems might work. As they remark in their final sentence, a real world context would requite elements from all four models.

Question 5: C

Abstract one argues that e-democracy will lead to more active civic engagement and democratic reform, which is viewed favourably. Abstract two does not have a view on whether changes to democracy are to be welcomed or not.

Question 6: B

Both articles suggest a blend of approaches is necessary for e-democracy. Article one states that e-democracy should be coupled with traditional participation methods and should not be separated from everyday operations of government – a blended approach. Article 2 states that any e-democracy may require elements from all four models – again, a blended approach.

Task Two
Question 7: D
The author says that animals make moral decisions based on emotions, and 'this holds true for human morality'.

Question 8: A
Even if there was data showing that animals were motivated by inner states this is irrelevant – this does not show that animas are moral.

Question 9: B
The author strongly rejects that the connection between animals is anything like human cognition. Humans have a 'theory of mind' and reflection, and animas run on instinct.

Question 10: C
The author presents a debate between those who think that animals have moral status and those who think they do not.

Question 11: D
This author states that emotions 'provide a window on adaptation' and so gives insights into evolution.

Question 12: A
The author gives the example of executing animals for immoral behaviour, something which is supposed to strike the reader as absurd.

Question 13: D
It was recently unacceptable to say that animals had no cognition. This view has now been fully accepted.
Question 14: C
The writer argues that differences between humans and animals are used to justify painful practices towards animals.

Task Three

Question 15: A

The implication is that this was a controversial approach. Dodds is apologetic for using anthropological material, but since that time this is a commonplace approach. This suggests it used to be controversial but no longer is.

Question 16: C

Anthropology is useful because it makes the Greeks seem strange to us – it is important to keep a sense of their 'otherness' and cultural anthropology helps us to do that.

Question 17: B

The writer concedes that anthropology could be useful for studying the Greeks because it 'also invokes similarities' which can be used to investigate universal features of societies. This is useful because his focus is on the similarities of Greek society and ours.

Question 18: C

The similarity he investigates is how we interpret our own and other people's feelings and actions – the manner in which we understand events and emotions.

Question 19:D

The author suggests it is hard for anthropologists to avoid assuming a different status from their subjects – there is an asymmetry between the anthropologist and the culture being studied.

Question 20: B

It's different in the case of studying the Greeks because the Greeks have an intimate connection with our lives and the view of ourselves.

Question 21:C

The new traditions do not cancel the fact that Greek past ,history, is the 'past of modernity'. This means that the importance of Greek history will not be undermined.

Question 22: A

The writer exploits a distinction between self understanding and self criticism. By studying the Ancient Greeks, we can work out ways in which our ideas may be wrong, which enables us to be more critical.

Question 23: D

Nietzsche uses 'untimely' to mean 'not fitting into current ways of thinking'. He does not want philology to 'act against the age', which implies he wants it to fit into current ways of thinking.

Question 24: B

The author specifically wants to study how the thought of the ancient Greeks is similar to ours in the modern world. In the final paragraph he wants to understand how our ideas are related to the ideas of the Greeks.

Task Four
Question 25: B
The hard boiled crime story is readily recognisable by readers – its hallmarks plunge us into a deeply familiar world whose features come out of collective imagination. It is not linked to ancient stories, it does not distort attitudes to crime, and there is no suggestion it is over simplified.

Question 26: A
The author discusses implications of the popularity of the genre. Its popularity means that the richness of the fiction is obscured.

Question 27: B
At the end of the paragraph the author mentions a diversity of artists who use the genre to pursue different ambitions. This diversity was mentioned previously – the author discusses 'the variety' of the crime narrative. There is no mention of negative critical reception, low status of writers, or the influence outside the USA.

Question 28: A
The author discusses the social and commercial factors that led to the genre. The social setting of Prohibition and over population led to a new type of crime writing, and the cheapness of the paper enabled millions of people to read them.

Question 29: B
The focus of paragraph four is to discuss how the hard boiled style changed the detective genre by making it more realistic. Whereas classic detectives, such as Sherlock Holmes, operated in an elaborate fantasy world of scheming aristocrats, the hard boiled detective dealt with more realistic crimes in a grimy urban setting.

Question 30: C
The author quotes Shaw to support his claim that the hard boiled style undermined the classic detective genre. Shaw states that the hard boiled characters bleed when they are wounded and aren't just 'dummies'. This builds on the overall point he makes in this paragraph.

Question 31: D
The leisure class and the Venetian vase are both pleasingly artificial. The 'vogue' was for the detective genre itself. The focus on the leisure class and vases has nothing to do with brilliant reasoning powers and elaborate schemes.

Question 32:D
In this paragraph the writer exposes the similarities between the hard boiled crime story and the detective fiction.

Question 33: B
Despite saying the crime novels were realistic, the author points out that very few writers had personal involvement in the criminal worlds they created. The assumption is that their realism stems from personal engagement, but it is just fiction.

Question 34: A
The author discusses the origins of certain underlying themes, such as the city as urban frontier. The two main types of influence, dime novels and Westerns, do not diverge but rather converge to form the hard boiled genre.

Question 35: A
The' popular fantasy' refers to the detective story which was previously popular and discussed in paragraph 4.

Question 36: C
The author explicitly mentions xenophobic suspicion due to the expansion of cities and cultural diversity – in other words, the multiplicity of nationalities was regarded as a threat. The author does not mention the inability of the government to keep order. There is no suggestion corporations had supreme power, and no indication that freedoms were being reversed.

Practice Paper A

<u>Task One</u>

Question 1: D
The authors complain that the existing literature lacks detail, lacks data analysis, and lacks sufficient attention to algorithms.

Question 2: A
The authors write that computers themselves are changing far more than demand for lawyers is.

Question 3: C
The reviewer believes that the book is too neoliberal, rather than too Marxist, and does not mention style or identity. They do however write that the book's flaws fatally undermine its argument.

Question 4: D
The author offers this critique in the second sentence, claiming it is the foundation of the book's argument.

Question 5: C
B is what they are arguing for – it is not an error. A is not an error but an assumption they make. D is a specific element of the error but is not the error itself. The error is that they think that professionalism can be conflated with the delivery of expertise which is too reductive.)

Question 6: B
Both take a critical analysis of automation. Abstract one thinks that automation is not as threatening as some make it out to be, and abstract two critiques assumptions that proponents of automation make.

Task Two

Question 7: D

All the others refer directly to The Equality Act, while Peter Dunne only refers to the Gender Recognition Act.

Question 8: D

Peter Dunne is most concerned with young transgender people, as his whole passage focuses on these concerns.

Question 9: B

Rosa Freedman mentions laws in Netherlands around gender identity in her closing sentence.

Question 10: C

Maureen O'Hara makes reference to the British Association of Gender Identity and the British Psychological Society.

Question 11: A

Alex Sharpe summarises the debate, putting forward pro and con positions separately.

Question 12: C

Maureen O'Hara refers to empirical evidence about the distribution of sex offenders.

Question 13: A

Alex Sharpe states her position in support of this in her opening sentence.

Question 14: B

Rosa Freedman compares changes in gender to those in nationality in the second paragraph.

Task Three

Question 15: C
The author says that the value of these attempts is things said 'by the way'. This suggests the authors do not succeed in finding a universal formula of beauty.

Question 16: D
He says these discussions help very little with all of the above.

Question 17: B.
The author is making the point that definitions of beauty are useless if we pitch them at too abstract a level.

Question 18: B
Pater states this clearly in the final sentence of the first paragraph.

Question 19: C
Pater states this in the second paragraph, that all qualities including beauty, are relative.

Question 20: C
The first step is to know one's impression of it according to the author.

Question 21: C
Pater emphasises that personal experience, primary data, in the most important thing by far in forming aesthetic judgments.

Question 22: B
Pater is laying out the kinds of questions one should ask when trying to understand the beaurty of a work of art.

Question 23: D
He says they are unprofitable, so not worth it. He says they may or may not have an answer. And he explains that questions about beauty in the abstract are metaphysical, so they may be abstract.

Question 24: B
Pater's aim is to instruct the student in how to appreciate art, and to understand beauty.

Task Four
Question 25: B
The objective correlative is the set of situations, objects, or events which create an emotion. The emotion relies on all being present, not just some of them.

Question 26: C
The purpose of the objective correlative is to evoke an emotional response in the reader.

Question 27: D
Eliot emphasises that the presence of the objective correlative is key to a successful tragedy.

Question 28: C
He is being ironic – nothing is really inevitable in the plays because it is all Shakespeare's choice.

Question 29: C
C is the correct answer. A is part of the problem, but not all of it. Both B and D are a good thing, and not present.

Question 30: D
They share the emotion of bafflement. Only Shakespeare suffers from B and only Hamlet has C. 'genuine' refers to the feeling of bafflement.

Question 31: B
A is incorrect – the writer thinks that even if the mother was made more evil this wouldn't solve the problem. The correct answer is B – his mother is insignificant, hence a minor character.

Question 32: C
He says that one excuse for hamlet's emotions would be if he was a teenager – but he is not.

Question 33: D
Eliot mentions all of the options offered.

Question 34: D
Eliot says we would need to know about all the options mentioned.

Question 35: A
Dissimulation is related to the word simulate, which means to fake or falsely recreate.

Question 36: A
Eliot's aim is to lay out his problems with *Hamlet*.

Practice Paper B

Task One

Question 1: C
He advocates that freedom of speech should be regarded like freedom of action. He denies that free speech has a special value, he thinks the court's approach to free speech cannot be applied to the rest of the polity, and he isn't impressed with autonomy based defences of free speech.

Question 2: C
The author states that only the problem of the epistemic arbiter poses a problem for speech regulation in the polity. This problem is referred to in the previous paragraph – the polity lacks an official referee. A and D are identified as problems, but they are not the main problem. B is a separate topic which is discussed later.

Question 3: B
The author explicitly states that free speech can be justifiably restricted in the case of defamation (A) and breach of the peace (D). He does think that hate speech is a problem and clashes with equality (c). However, the author doesn't indicate any problem with spreading libertarian ideas.

Question 4: D
The author states that freedom of expression can clash with the goals of equality. It's not A – the fourteenth amendment is said to sit side by side with free speech. And it's not B or C – these are the products of free speech but don't clash with it.

Question 5: A
Neither. Both think that freedom of speech should be restricted in some way.

Question 6: C
Abstract one. The author explicitly compares speech regulation in court to the polity at large. The author of abstract two does discuss findings of the Supreme court, but this is not the same thing as discussing how the institution of the court regulates speech within the court itself.

Task Two

Question 7: D
Cowen suggests this in his opening sentence.

Question 8: C
Caplan's passage is primarily concerned with the economically irrational preferences of voters.

Question 9: B
Given that the voting age is 18 in most parts of the world, Runciman's suggestion of lowering it to 6 is intended to seem initially absurd.

Question 10: A
Scott Cato gives a number of specific examples in her passage, and none of the other writers favour changing the voting age to 16 specifically.

Question 11: C
Caplan is very pessimistic about voters, who he sees as biased and irrational.

Question 12: D
Cowen pokes fun at the seriousness with which elections are treated when he writes "and I'm glad that we have a whole day devoted to this important issue.", as he thinks the issue is taken too seriously by most people.

Question 13: B
Runciman puts considerable emphasis on the clash between generations throughout his passage.

Question 14: D
Cowen says that you shouldn't vote if you don't like it, or don't know which candidate to choose.

Task Three

Question 15: D
He points out the representatives are accused of 'selling their voices', which is bribery. Voltaire does say there are no differences, but later clarifies this by conceding one. He denies they have similar ideas about good and evil. Rome and England do both have a senate, but the main clause of the sentence is concerned with the members of the senate not the senate itself.

Question 16: C
He later says these kinds of quarrels are 'trifling 'which means trivial. They aren't serious. He thinks that religious war itself is a folly and abomination, not the quarrels which lead to war"

Question 17: D
They won't be silly enough to have a war because they have 'grown wiser at their own expense', which is another way of saying they have learned a lesson after suffering losses. There is no indication the English no longer have trifling quarrels. He states they don't care to murder each other over syllogisms, not that they don't care about syllogisms. And the sects are no longer silly precisely because they have learned their lesson.

Question 18: A
The author states that the English are the only people who can limit the power of the king by resisting him. This means the king does not have unlimited power. The author states the king is restrained from committing evil, there are no vassals (serfs), and the people share in the government.

Question 19: C
The only way to keep the plebians out of the administration was to send them to foreign wars. A isn't correct – the Romans eventually ended up in slavery but the patricians did not enslave the plebians. D) we are told didn't happen. B) is an description of their conflict, but doesn't explain how the plebians were kept away from government

Question 20: B
The problem with the conflict is that there is no balance between the two powers and nothing to mediate between them. So having a third branch of government would help the situation.

Question 21: D
Levity means 'light hearted', or 'flippant'. It is the opposite of serious.

Question 22: D
Conquest, domination, and repression of others are all seen as necessary to glory by the author.

Question 23: A
The author writes "their divisions sunk them into slavery."

Question 24: B
In broad terms, the main aim is B – to compare the similarities between the Romans and the English.

Task Four

Question 25: C
He states it has among its alumni the most distinguished scholars, so he is speaking about alumni only.

Question 26: B
All of the other positions are mentioned in the text.

Question 27: C
The locations are listed at the top of the third paragraph.

Question 28: D
The author says 'of course' he has no counsel (advice) to offer the men, and this is probably because the author is not religious and so does not have much useful advice to give them. However, from the text itself there is no apparent reason why he has no counsel to offer them.

Question 29: C
He says they are 'affectionate and gregarious' in their ways. He says he met a few men who were in the mood to make sacrifices, but this doesn't describe their personality.

Question 30: D
The author says that Cambridge men and Oxford men are equally affectionate but the Oxford men have more polished manners than Cambridge men.

Question 31: B
He isn't being nostalgic, because he hasn't been here before. There is nothing humorous in his description, and he isn't poking fun at the situation.

Question 32: D
It means 'custom' – he contrasts' use and wont with 'good nature' so it cannot mean the same thing as nature/character/personality.

Question 33: B
He says this is 'still more descriptive' of their good nature, which means this is the most pressing reason to think they are good natured.

Question 34: D
You can't tell. He says that Cambridge has the advantage over Oxford but this doesn't mean he prefers it. He doesn't give an indication in the text about which he personally prefers.

Question 35: A
He isn't overly worshipful in his praise , nor is he critical or contemptuous. He doesn't appear confused by the customs of the English. The best word is 'positive'

Question 36: C
The author's goal is to not his thoughts on England generally, as shown by the brief attention given to each subject in the passage. One can reasonably suppose this from the title of the work from which this piece is taken, *English Traits*.

Practice Paper C

Task One

Question 1: C
The writers infer that countries with smaller populations, which can raise smaller armies, are less of a threat to democratic neighbours.

Question 2: D
When a country feels threatened, its volunteer military forces will be larger.

Question 3: A
D isn't an assumption because the author states it outright. There is nothing to imply in the text that rich offspring are better fighters than poor people, or that they like to fight in the war -in fact, later the author points out that the rich offspring will seek to defer deployment. The assumption is A – poor people are less able to protest and campaign against wars. Rich and well connected people are better at this than poor people.

Question 4: C
The model predicts C, because the cost of stopping the war is very high overall, whereas the cost of helping one person dodge the draft is very low. Consequently, it makes more rational sense to focus your efforts on helping your son dodge the draft that on protesting the war as a whole.

Question 5: D
Abstract one just presents facts about conscription whereas abstract two critiques an argument in favour of conscription.

Question 6: B
Both. Abstract one most obviously uses a cross country data set which is empirical evidence. Abstract 2 references empirical evidence from Vietnam at the very end.

Task Two

Question 7: C
De Grauwe explicitly states the at the start of his second paragraph.

Question 8: A
Downey writes that automation lowers the skill level required for a job, but does not eliminate that job. None of the other writers mention automation.

Question 9: D
Wright says that government benefits are more effective than minimum wage increases, as the resilience of the UK unemployment rate in 2008-10 showed.

Question 10: D
Wright says that the minimum wage should be tailored to the needs of different kinds of household.

Question 11: B
Tabbarok corrects a misconception around minimum wages, arguing that wages and overall compensation, which includes bonuses, can be quite different.

Question 12: C
De Grauwe cites the track record of the minimum wage at avoiding political extremism and combating inequality.

Question 13: B
Although all the writers refer to the historical record, only Tabbarok uses the adverb recently in describing his example.

Question 14: D
Wright discusses poverty throughout his passage, while the others do not mention it, or discuss inequality.

Task Three

Question 15: D
A person who has these things will have 'little more to wish for' – and so will not need much else to be happy. A is a common misreading ("has a little more to wish for), B is based on a misreading of 'need' to mean desire, and C is contradicted by the text)

Question 16: B
The author states that our happiness and misery is mostly of our own making. This means we do have some control, so B is false. He does think that a 'full description of a happy state' is having a healthy mind and body, so he agrees with A. He also thinks that those without wise minds can never make good choices, so would agree with the converse which is C. He directly states D.

Question 17: D
'Well fram'd by nature' refers to traits that some humans are naturally born with. The author does not mention beauty. B contradicts the idea of it being natural, as opposed to acquired. C is a consequence of being well framed by nature but doesn't explain what it means.

Question 18: C
Education. Nine-tenths of what makes us good or evil etc is education, according to Locke. The men affected mostly by nature are rare.

Question 19: C
He talks about tiny insensible causes having big effects and relates this to moving the water of a river into a different course with a gentle push of the hand. He isn't talking generally about human life. Education is not analogous to a river. D is far too literal a reading.

Question 20: D
The following sentences make clear the contrast between the water of the mind, and the clay cottage of the body.

Question 21: B
He says that the minds of children turn this way or that like flowing water. The opposite of this is 'constant' so it's not D. He doesn't claim that children are irrational, and this doesn't fit the water analogy. Water flows, but the main emphasis about children's mind is that they move one way then the other so C isn't the best description.

Question 22: C
He states that the necessity of health to our business and happiness doesn't require any proof, as it is obvious from to everyone from experience.

Question 23: C
The phrase means "I will get the discussion of bodily health over and done with quickly because it has very narrow scope – in short, there isn't much to talk about." A is incorrect. 'lying' does not refer to dishonesty. B confuses the term 'compass' meaning scope with a physical compass. D doesn't capture the meaning. Students may be tripped up if they fail to appreciate this old fashioned metaphor.

Question 24: A
In every paragraph the author talks about the body and mind and its workings/cultivation. B is too narrow because he mentions the body as well. He only briefly mentions happiness and natural geniuses.

Task Four

Question 25: D
All the above reasons are mentioned at some point in the passage.

Question 26: D
The author states that the necessary conditions for love at first sight and weddings within a week are romance and the ideal of Lochinvar. It follows that if these don't' exist there can be no shotgun weddings according to the author.

Question 27: C
Sex and ankles used to be hidden from view, now they are common place and less mysterious and alluring.

Question 28: B
The biggest difference is the "unreserved frankness" between men and women. This means they are more open with each other.

Question 29: A
It's not D – she isn't using these quotation marks in a citational sense. Quote marks can be used to express sarcasm or to emphasise disagreement, but she seems to be reporting as a matter of fact what these conventions used to be called. A is the best answer – she is wanting to highlight the absurdity of the conventions.

Question 30: B
She is sceptical because she doubts the young man is really 'devoted' at all – she thinks they are just playing a role.

Question 31: C
It is more authentic now than in the past.

Question 32: B
She mentions them going to balls but discusses this in the context of them sitting together for supper. They are said to dance at their houses.

Question 33: D
All the other advantages of the group habit are mentioned.

Question 34: D
The passage emphasises that they are 'friends' so it's not romantic The passage also uses the word natural and intimate to refer to the relationship so platonic must mean 'friendly'.

Question 35: B
The author in paragraph one says it is wiser to delay marriage. She thinks the dating style of 25 years ago is stuffy. She much prefers courtship today and emphasises women and men becoming friends before marriage.

Question 36: A
It is clear, both from the text itself and the title, that the aim of the text is to discuss changes in attitude towards courtship and engagement.

Practice Paper D

Task One

Question 1: C

Just as Ford was the leader in mass assembly, so too is Google the leader in surveillance capitalism.

Question 2: D

All the attributes of 'The Big Other' listed are mentioned in the first abstract.

Question 3: B

All the others are mentioned and kinds of domination in the second abstract.

Question 4: A

The writer explicitly states that it is through US control of access to digital technologies that colonialism is being repeated.

Question 5: A

Neither. Both abstracts are critical of it.

Question 6: B

While abstract 2 focuses the most on colonial control, abstract 2 also focuses on control from the 'big other'

Task Two

Question 7: B
Tabbarok argues that migration is a human right, saying that it is a basic liberty.

Question 8: D
Adler writes that control over borders is one of the key rights of the nation.

Question 9: A
Shiller argues that in the future, we will see the very idea of borders between countries as being morally wrong.

Question 10: A
Shiller takes a historical approach, focusing on intellectual revolutions of centuries past.

Question 11: C
Cowen addresses critics of open borders, who he argues concentrate too much on the idea of borders.

Question 12: C
Cowen argues that the cost of living in a country, not the ease of immigration to it, is the key question.

Question 13: A
Shiller hypothesises that more people will be part of a gloablised economy with large transnational firms in the future.

Question 14: D
Adler believes that tough border control is permissible, as control of borders is a fundamental right of the nation state.

Task Three

Question 15: C
The author states that we can perceive the imitation and on that principle are pleased with it. The closest answer is C. D isn't an explanation, there is no hint that he thinks we enjoy real tragedies, and the imperfection is the reason we spot the imitation not why we enjoy it.

Question 16: D
The writer states that the only difference between the two is that we get more pleasure from imitated tragedies. The student must go with what is written exactly in the text, even though A, B, and C may very well be real differences between the two earthquakes.

Question 17: B
Burke is clear that the pleasure of tragedy doesn't just derive from it being fictional. He says that this sour grapes vision of art is mistaken.

Question 18: D
Burke would agree that tragedy is more powerful when it more closely resembles reality.

Question 19: A
Based on his comparison between the perfect play and the execution he would agree with A.

Question 20: C
He says that we enjoy watching tragedies, like a fire, even though we would never dream about actually starting a fire ourselves.

Question 21: C
A sophism is a faulty or fallacious argument, so C. It doesn't mean error – he already said 'mistake' in the sentence, so not A.

Question 22: A
Burke argues that we need some distance from tragic events if we are to enjoy and experience them as fiction.

Question 23: C
Describing 'being alive' as the cause of death is absurd according to Burke, as it is true by definition, therefore not an insight.

Question 24: D
Burke wishes to explore in this passage why we react so differently to fictional and real tragedy.

Task Four

Question 25: D
He says animals can 'infer, which is a kind of reasoning. Animals learn from experience, just like humans, and they also grasp cause and effect.

Question 26: D
The writer says that animals know the basic properties of objects, so B. the animals also know the nature of objects, so A, and the effects of objects, so C. But he doesn't say anything about more abstract concepts so d is the odd one out.

Question 27: D
Inexperience can mean the same thing as naïve, and sagacity refers to wisdom. 'ignorance' is more akin to being unknowledgable than stupid. 'Cunning' also refers to clever, and not deceitful.

Question 28: C
The author already mentioned that older animals know the effects of fire, so D is true. The young cat is not like the wise horse who knows how to jump, and the old rat will have learned from experience that there is a trap. The author says that young racedogs haven't learned to pace themselves yet, so he wouldn't agree with C.

Question 29: D
He says animals learn best through the correct application of reward and punishment. He never says that reward is the best option.

Question 30: A
The questions are rhetorical and are designed to get the reader to agree with him.

Question 31: C
He is continuing his thesis about animal education in general. He isn't taking just about dogs, so not C, and he does not continue the topic about older/young animals. The effects of discipline has just been introduced for the first time and is further evidence for his education theory.

Question 32: D
Hume's theory is that animals will infer some fact beyond what their senses tell them via experience and association. A to C all involve association and are similar to his previous examples.

Question 33: B
The purpose of this passage is to educate the reader about his theory of education and experience. It isn't funny. Polemics are a strong written attack on something and he doesn't attack anything in this piece. He isn't being personally reflective either. B is the best choice.

Question 34: D
All of these animals are referred to at least once in the passage, which is not the case for the other options.

Question 35: B
D is too broad – he does highlight the importance of observation, but the context is more to do with animals. C is too narrow, as is A, so the answer is B.

Question 36: B
He references multiple times that animals infer, so they can reason. He denies that animals mainly get by via innate knowledge.

Anglo Saxon, Norse, and Celtic

Specimen Paper

How could an historian approach this poem as a source for the history of Anglo-Saxon England?

Your introduction will outline the body of your discussion in brief, listing in summary what major points the essay will require you to cover, and how you will go about answering them. You may want to define what it means to look at the source as a historian, rather than a literary scholar or a more general reader. What are you looking for as a historian? What are you trying to understand about the time in question? E.g. How they lived, what they thought, what they valued, what events took place. Make a statement about what you will explore below.

The body of your essay will briefly discuss each issue you raise. These issues will be relevant in most cases to any historical source a student might read, which is why the question stresses the relative unimportance of foreknowledge of the text. When you are discussing a historical source in a very general way it is a good rule of thumb to write a three-part answer for each point you make. This three-part answer will *Address* an issue, *Relate* the evidence, then draw *Conclusions*, you may remember this as the *ARC* rule. It is then up to you to argue your case convincingly and draw as much out of a text as you possibly can.

In order to make a convincing case, each point you make must use information directly from the text as an example. If, for example, you are discussing the disposition of the writer towards the characters in the text, you could draw upon the specific line *'king Of Wessex, prince among earls and patron Of heroes, and his noble brother, Edmund'* as evidence that the writer wants to give a positive impression of King Athelstan. Once you have raised the issue and given evidence, you can then discuss the possible reasons for the writers allegiance, and what it tells you about a) the writer, b) King Athelstan, and c) the drawbacks of using the *Chronicle* as a source. You are only limited by your imagination- but try to stick to the three-part schema as much as possible so that every point you make has some textual evidence supporting it.

Some potential themes to address within this specific text include: the authors' social-standing, his employment, his political and religious views, when in history he was writing relative to the events described, whether there is any evidence of direct or familial bond with the parties in the text, whether he was likely to have any first-hand experience of the events related, if he did not have any first-hand experience, what he had read, etc. Yu may also ask questions about the poetic nature of the text. Does the desire to entertain affect the narratives historic value? How does it? Where in the text is there evidence of hyperbole or imagination? For example the lines: *'All the Scots and the shipborne Vikings, Ran or drowned in blood, dropped To a landlocked fate as the glorious sun Went gliding over the earth like a candle'*, gives us less detail about the battle than maybe we would like, because the author has opted for a more poetic or evocative way of depicting the scene.
Explore as many issues as you can in the time allowed.

The conclusion of your essay will condense your conclusions about the evidence discussed above into a short paragraph. Ensure you use succinct language, avoid over-explanation and flowery prose. From the bulk of the evidence you have explored, what general statements can you make about a Historians use of the text?

With reference to this poem, discuss the uses that a literary scholar could make of a poem on a historical topic.

Question two will follow a similar schematic, but the nature of the questions you must ask about the text are different. In the introduction you may want to, as above summarise what you are about to do in the body of the essay and define what a literary scholar looks for in a text versus a historian or general reader. The literary scholar may be more focused on the form of the poem, it's rhythm and metre, it's poetic imagery and what it tells us about history of the English language.

For this question the student will want to consider how the blending of historical and artistic goals effects. Among the themes you might consider are, how the use of poetic devices structures the text, is the poem less creative than it could be because its primary function is to explain history? Is the poem an attempt to reproduce a story or narrative, or does it aim to evoke a feeling of time a place? Are there any ways in which the poems use of poetic language obscures the literal meaning? What has the writer prioritized during his composition?

As you discuss these points draw on the text where you can. For example, you may want to consider the structure and devices used in the poems, and what this tells you about the early history of English poetry. All the animals mentioned in the narrative have epithets: *'the grey-feathered eagle, splashed white On his tail, to the greedy war-hawk and the grey-flanked Forest wolf'*. Is this writing reflective of an earlier, or contemporary oral tradition? If so, how can you see this in the text? Is there repetition or are epithets used in such a way that makes the text more memorable?

Other themes you may want to elaborate on are how are early English values and ideas of virtue promoted by the texts' panegyric style? What other poetic devices are used in the text; does it use simile or metaphor? If it does not, is this surprising? How useful is the text as a landmark piece of poetry-writing in a period without much writing? Is it likely to be typical or atypical of other early English writing?

In the final paragraph of the essay you may wish to conclude your views on what the text tells you about early English poetry.

Sample Paper A

How might a historian go about verifying detail contained in texts of this kind?

This question is asking you to think more broadly about the kinds of evidence historians use. This requires you to go beyond just examining the source at hand. In your introduction you may want to make a statement about the limits of using any one sources and how you will explore below the different kinds of evidence Historians need to build a complete picture of the past. You may want to list these in brief.

Comb through the text you are presented with and draw out as many different sorts of details as you can. For each type of detail consider how other sources, literary or archaeological may shed light-on or contradict the narrative. Use evidence directly from the text and discuss.

The text makes references to letters written to the Romans about the problems in Britain, is it possible these letters still exist or are referenced elsewhere? Some of the narrative concerns the history of the appointment of British bishops, there may be a record of this in the Vatican. The passages about the Hunnic invasions are well recorded in multiple sources throughout the Mediterranean. Finally consider the role of the archaeological record in confirming the movements of different peoples around Europe. A sudden change in the style of objects such as jewellery, weaponry and armour can be read as a sign of a different group or tribe invading a region, although it may also reflect trade and community. The abandonment of settlements is also frequently used as evidence of war and famine.

It is worth contrasting verifiable details with any details you do not believe are verifiable or belong to the opinion of the author only. If you were going to discuss Bede's explanation of famine you may want to draw upon the lines : *'In the meantime, on a sudden, a grievous plague fell upon that corrupt generation, which soon destroyed such numbers of them, that the living scarcely availed to bury the dead'* Bede here makes reference to the 'corrupt generation', as a form of explanation for Britain's' troubles. Is his belief debauchery hastened Britain's problems purely conjecture built on religious belief? Or has he perhaps drawn this idea from another ecclesiastical writer? Is there likely to be any evidence in a change in behaviour that lead him to believe in a 'corrupt generation'?

Reiterate in your conclusion the range of outside evidence you have used.

How might Bede's priorities as a historian have been different from those of historians today?

In the introduction you may want to make a statement that summarises in broad strokes the differing aims of a modern historians and Bede. E.g. 'The aims of Bede are arguably grounded in the need for religious and historical myth-making in contrast to a modern historians' need for clarity, and fact-finding.' Make a bold statement about the direction your argument will take.

There are many issues you might consider when thinking about the authorship of a historical piece, and the authors intention. As suggested by the title, Bede prioritised the history of the English church, and the nations move towards Christianity, over other historical topics. Although this may usefully reveal facts about the English Church, it is also means he uses religious explanations for historical events, as when he says *'Nor were the laity only guilty of these things, but even our Lord's own flock, with its shepherds, casting off the easy yoke of Christ, gave themselves up to drunkenness, enmity, quarrels, strife, envy, and other such sins.'* This, and examples like this can be used to illustrate Bede's focus on belief, faith, and religion. He even uses it to explain events as when he says 'as the event plainly showed, was brought about by the Lord's will, that evil might fall upon them for their wicked deeds.'

You may also find examples in which the aims and methods of Bedes's historical writing is similar to that of a modern historians, for example at one point in the text he says : ' *To him the wretched remnant of the Britons sent a letter, which began thus:—"To Aetius, thrice Consul, the groans of the Britons."'*, which suggest Bede may have actually researched and found letters to build his history.

In the conclusion present a brief overview of what you have just argued as you did in the introduction.

Sample Paper B

Did Monmouth believe that he was recording facts in this passage? If not, why not?

In your introduction you will give an overview of broadly where your argument is likely to go. If you believe Monmouth did in fact think he was recording facts, you will stress this in the introduction. If you believe it is impossible to say you may say this also. The introduction serves to direct the reader as to where your argument is leading them.

The body of your essay will address issues of intention, and the difficulty of proving the intention of an author from a text. Wherever possible draw direct examples from the passage you are given to illustrate the point you are making. Even if you are arguing strongly for, or strongly against the view Monmouth believed he was writing facts, you must include where possible evidence you perceive to go against your general argument and address these arguments. Your essays must always weigh up the balance of evidence that is there, rather than trying to trick the reader, or ignore alternate viewpoints.

You may want to bring in your knowledge of history here to illustrate how the story Merlin tells in the text alludes to real events Monmouth would have known about; for example the lines :'*The house of Romulus shall dread his courage, and his end shall be doubtful.*' Makes a clear allusion to the fall of Rome. You may want to consider the entertainment value of telling the history of Britain in a metaphorical and fantastical way and see some humour in the text. If Monmouth is creating a fable here, is there some benefit from his point of view, of claiming certain events were fated or inevitable? Does the myth he told depict the kings of his own time in an unfavourable light? If he did not invent the story in the narrative, is he merely repeating a story he had read elsewhere? Where is it likely to have come from? From a chronicle, or from oral histories? Were his own sources lacking in credibility leaving him little choice in the stories he could report?

As well as exploring reasons to doubt the earnestness of the narrative, you should explore reasons he may have believed what he was saying was true. This involves addressing issues surrounding myth and belief in the 12th century. Dragons are a popular part of medieval folklore, and you could argue people were more credulous at that time. Many peoples in the past have also believed events were predestined or fated.

In the conclusion you will want to reiterate briefly your overall view and summarise why there is not enough evidence to defend the contrary view, or if you believe it is impossible to know one way or the other you may want to state that in your final paragraph.

What does the interweaving of factual and fictional characters suggest about pre-modern history writing?

The introduction will make a statement about what you will argue is the main problem or problems with the interweaving of fact and fiction in history writing for a modern reader. You may also want to draw attention to the fact it usefully tells us something about the values and intellectual climate of the time.

In the body of your essay draw up a list of things you believe the blending of genres in the past tells us about the past itself. This specific question is not asking for an argument leading in any one direction but is pushing you to produce as many questions as you can from a limited amount of information.

Does it raise questions about the nature of belief at the time? Of where the burden of truth lies? Did they value truth less than us? Why? What role does myth have in creating national identity? How does the author use symbolism (the red and white dragons) to create a compelling story? Is it possible to argue Monmouth wanted to entertain rather than investigate? Does the author intend to portray the real characters in a certain light which benefits from the weaving of fact with fiction? Does it make the historical figures seem grader or more heroic, or crueller and more monstrous? How does exaggeration and hyperbole distort an dramatize the narrative? Where possible draw directly from the text direct evidence to illustrate your claims. There are several angles you may want to take on this subject, try to address as many as you can in the time allowed.

Themes you might consider include

In the conclusion summarise the issues raised in your essay as eloquently as you can. Perhaps you can list multiple reasons Monmouth would not worry about distinguishing between fact and fiction.

<u>Sample Paper C</u>

What choices has the translator made in this version of the text? Why do you think he has made them?

Begin by summarising the major themes you will address in the body of your essay, which questions will you raise about the translation? Be as succinct as possible.

In the body of the essay you will want to discuss the make-up of the poem using references from sections of the text. Begin by asking basic questions. Is the translation in poetry or prose? Is it in rhyme? What devices has the poet used in the poem and why? For example the same character has multiple epithets, such as *'sturdy Scyld'* or *'winsome sclyde'*. Why has the translator done this? What does it make yo think of? The translator has also made heavy use of alliteration: *'with weapons of war and weeds of battle, with breastplate and blade: on his bosom lay'*. Why might the translator have chosen these repetitive devices? What effects do they have on you when you read it, and what rhythm do they give to the narrative? Is it more memorable or evocative? Is the word choice completely modern, or is it antiquated? Do you think thee features are true to the original? How does the translator give an impression of the text's antiquity? For instance in the line: *'High o'er his head they hoist the standard'*, why has the writer chosen o'er rather than over?

Having drawn out what you can from the text stylistically consider how this affects your reading of it. Does it evoke an antiquated feeling that makes you think of the Old English original? Does it fail to do this?

To summarise make a brief assessment of what you have discussed. Has the translator succeeded in his aims? What are his aims? What benefit has the translation provided over other possible translation styles, what drawbacks?

The authorship of Beowulf is unknown. What challenges might this pose for a literature student studying the poem? And for a historian? Are these challenges different?

This is a two-part question that requires a two-part answer, your introduction should flag up in brief the thematic differences between a literary and historical appraisal of Beowulf, and state how you wish to address these issues below.

This question asks you to address issues of historicity, as well as literary history. Every time you raise an issue, with an example from the text, assess the issue from a historical then literary perspective, then contrast your answers. Follow this formula throughout. Firstly, you may want to address the form of the narrative. Is the poet a bard, concerned only with telling a story? Is the poet an early kind of chronicler, whose stories happen to dip into myth but may contain grains of truth? What is the writer's intention? Next you may want to address the chronology of the story. What date was the poet writing? Can we even know? Did the poet intend to set the story in the recent or distant past? If it was the recent past, what small details about the time period can we draw from the narrative? If the distant past, would the poet have some knowledge of the time period he is talking about at a distance? Will the details reflect his own time rather than the era he is talking about, or has he deliberately chosen antiquated ideas and practices the audience would recognise as old? Finally, what does the poem tell you about contemporary values? What was considered heroic? Honourable? Worthy of putting into writing? With each question you raise, support the answer with a piece of text if possible, and then compare a historian and literature student's viewpoint. For example we know from the lines *'Lo, praise of the prowess of people-kings of spear-armed Danes, in days long sped, we have heard, and what honor the athelings won!'* the author is referring to the past, but we don't know how long ago he is referring to. This an issue for a historian because we do not know how faithfully he is reproducing an image of an imagined past. It is less of an issue for a literature student who may be more interested in how the writer evokes the past, than he is with an actual timeline.

To conclude you may want to give your personal assessment of how the text works both as a historical source and a piece of literature. For example, you may conclude Beowulf's use as a source is limited, but it sheds a lot of light on the development of the English Language. Show how your reasoning has led you to make conclusions about both sides of the question asked. If you feel the answer is complex and multifaceted do not be afraid to say that.

Sample Paper D

Why might an author decide to attempt a project such as this? Why might they prioritise this kind of work?

In the introduction make a statement about what sort of project you believe is being attempted by the author, and any questions this raises, you will then address these questions below.

This question is asking you to identify what themes and feelings the author is trying to provoke in his reader. The work is antiquated, why would somebody want to write something that promotes the past? Is there an element of nationalism, or sentimentality/nostalgia at play? Why? How can you illustrate this with examples from the text? The text quoted in the example contains a creation myth *'Ukko is the first creator. Ukko, maker of the heavens, Cut apart the air and water, Ere was born the metal, iron.'* Why would a writer want to revisit an ancient and non-Christian creation story? You may also want to contrast the use of folklore with other types of writing. Does the text celebrate one thing to reject another? What would it mean in contrast to celebrating modernity? Why might the author not want to do this? In the text the author makes reference to themes of magic, and heroism : *"Tell me who thou art of heroes, Who of all the great magicians?'*, what sort of feelings does this mythmaking inspire? Can you think of a comparable project in the English language?

Write a statement about what themes your investigation has uncovered. Does one particular theme stick out to you as a motive? Do none?

What can we learn about Finnish identity from a work like this? What does it mean for a modern author to write a consciously old-fashioned work such as this?

In the introduction you may want to raise questions about how much we can learn about Finnish identity from a single author. State any themes you will address below, such as sentimentality, the reasons for that sentimentality, a need for old-fashioned values at the time author is writing etc.

Your essay will raise a series of questions grounded in the text about what it is this specific time period evokes. With each example given you may then address why you would want to evoke that feeling. You can draw on personal knowledge of the 19th century when the piece was written, as well as your knowledge of the time period being depicted.

This question asks you to look at Finnish perception of their own heritage, but because we may say the authors intentions are unknowable this gives you licence to imagine any number of motivations. What does the author seek to express or romanticise? Try to draw out imagery and detail from the text where possible. For example you may want to raise a point about the imagery at play in the writing, such as: *'These were mothers of the iron, And of steel of bright-blue color. Tremblingly they walked the heavens, Walked the clouds with silver linings'* The author here uses myth to show typically grey, grim Finnish weather in a beautiful and characterful way.

You may wish to raise questions about the historical themes the text reminds you of. Does it remind you of any other kinds or writing, such as epic or oral poetry? What can you infer from this about the authors intentions in the project? What period of Finnish history is taking centre stage in the poem, and why would it be source of focus? Is there more textual or archaeological evidence from the period depicted than other periods of Finnish history, or was it a period of identity building? Does it evoke a period where Finnish identity is more distinct from its neighbours? Are the pre-Christian themes an attempt at a revival of pre-Christian values and ideas such as magic and heroic virtues?

Write a brief statement about what you believe you have convincingly argued the writer is trying to do, and how he achieves that.

Asian and Middle Eastern Studies

<u>Specimen Paper</u>

What is at stake in these incidents, and what is your position? Should be not be allowed to dress up as 'Others' or are we going too far in restricting people's freedom of expression? Make sure to justify your position.

The introduction should give a summary of the extract's position, and introduce your response to the question. In doing so, you should be able to suggest what the stakes are. For example, that this is about more than 'dressing up', rather it is about the right of one culture to have authority and agency, the power dynamics at work given these examples consider white/European/American participants appropriating the cultures of people of colour/previously colonised peoples. A good introduction will also indicate how you will structure the essay, and give a clear sense of the direction.

In the body of the essay illustrate your argument and response with examples – a good point of departure is those given in the extract.

Mexican sombreros – you could use this example to point out the inequality between an elite university like Bowdoin and people of Mexican origin, and draw on wider knowledge by pointing out the particular persecution of Mexicans in contemporary America as a result of Donald Trump's policies. A close reading of the text will also be useful – for example pointing out the phrase 'white person's prerogative' as an indicator of this racial power inequality. Here, the safety and security of an entire population group has the potential to be undermined if it continues to be trivialised – clearly the stakes are about more than simply 'dressing up.'

Kimonos – this example could be utilised to indicate the ways in which cultural appropriation diminishes the original meaning of something. For example, taking a selfie in a kimono could be seen as disrespectful to the original significance of the kimono in Japanese society. It could also be used as an example of how objects from 'Other' cultures are seen as fashion statements and are exoticized. Wider knowledge could again be used here, for example the fashion for French artists in Monet's day to be inspired by Japan.

Mikado – this example could be used to suggest how things that were acceptable in one time period no longer have to be acceptable. Simply because Gilbert and Sullivan wrote a popular opera about Japan, does not mean that their approach to Japanese culture was respectful, and that does not mean that we are not allowed to criticise it now given our new contemporary sensibilities.

Conversely, you could use these examples to suggest that these are all trivial things that do not amount to racial discrimination, and focus in on the author's repeated mention of 'liberal arts colleges' to indicate that the furore surrounding cultural appropriation is little more than elite students trying to cause a commotion.

Your conclusion should answer the question in a concise focused manner, clearly expressing your opinion.

<u>Sample Paper A</u>

What distinctions does Deng draw in this speech? What are the implications for China's position relative to the rest of the world? What does government with Chinese characteristics mean today?

In the introduction, raise the fact that Deng raises a lot of binary oppositions in his speech, which help to position China in relation to the rest of the world. For example, communism vs. capitalism, east vs. west, old vs. new. Combined, these oppositions help create a sense of the particularly Chinese approach to government under socialism.

In the body of the essay, work through major themes from the text – using examples – in order to demonstrate what exactly is meant by government with Chinese characteristics.

Communism vs. Capitalism. Deng delivered this speech in 1984, at the height of the Cold War. This immediately puts China in opposition to the West (ie. America), to be therefore met with caution and suspicion. It would be possible to suggest that, in spite of China's increased move away from socialism and its huge economic prowess, this suspicion has remained and has led to the country remaining on the fringes of geopolitics.

East vs. West. In specifying a Chinese approach to government, Deng is deliberately positioning China as separate to other world powers. In other words, China has no interest in becoming like the USA, or indeed the USSR. Deng does however note China's closed-door policy as a main reason for the country's backwardness; this perhaps implicitly argues for less of an ideological distinction between China and the West than Western countries might assume.

Old vs. New. Deng calls for a specific definition of socialism that was not held in the past, and in doing so rhetorically heralds in a new age of Chinese government. There is a sense of a shift and of new beginnings for the country. China's rapid development since 1984 to become a major player in technological and economic innovation could be used as an example of the impact of this new age.

Other distinctions could include socialism vs. Marxism, industrial vs. agricultural, open vs. closed.

Conclusion; this is a complex question that asks you to balance a lot of different moving parts. Emphasise that China's position at the intersection of these distinctions and dichotomies is part of what gives it a particularly 'Chinese' characteristic.

Sample Paper B

What do we learn about Chinese family culture from this passage? What general principles are suggested by Jian's stratagem?

This question has two parts, but can be answered simply by picking out major themes about Chinese family culture, and then their overlap with Jian's principles. In the introduction, it would be useful to highlight some of these themes (honour, age hierarchy, obedience etc) and argue that these notions of family apply equally to Jian's military strategy – this itself is interesting as it tells us how the two areas have a lot in common.

It would be most effective to choose three themes highlighted in the text, and to structure the essay accordingly. For example:

Obedience – Sun Ce states that he will follow his father into battle because 'After all, I am your son.' This indicates the power and honour given to father's, and constructs the family as an almost militaristic operation. This notion is echoed by Jian's successive orders to his troops, and his requirement that they all shoot 'the arrows in unison'. In the extract, family and army operate on strict discipline and obedience.

Honour – The opening paragraph makes pains to indicate the heritage of Jian's children, the use of their style names and the emphasise of their mother as a 'Lady' indicates that hierarchy and lineage is important. Again this sentiment is echoed in Jian's military strategy; for example, he focuses on the need to 'avenge a slight' and gain retribution.

Hierarchy – We learn about Jian's children in age order, just as they give their allegiance in the same order. It is also clear that Jing's uncertainty about battle becomes irrelevant given his older brother Jian disagrees – Jian is clearly the decision maker, and the use of 'Younger Brother' and 'Older Brother' emphasise this. The echo between familiar honour (protecting one's family etc), and honour in battle, again reiterates the parallels we can draw between Chinese family culture and military culture.

Other possible themes could be patriarchy (the daughter's and wives are overlooked), territory, dominance etc.

The conclusion would summarise these themes, and reiterate the argument that there are useful parallels between Chinese military and family culture, of which this extract is a strong example.

Sample Paper C

What lessons about the nature of colonialism might be drawn from the experience of Hong Kong? How have Western views of the handover changed since 1997?

Your introduction should acknowledge that this question is asking you extrapolate from the text, and then apply your wider general knowledge. It would be useful to show that you understand what is meant by 'colonialism', and how Hong Kong differed in colonial nature to countries such as India. Your introduction should also outline how you intend to structure your response.

The body of the essay will focus in on a few key colonial themes as indicated in the text, before trying to situate that in the context of how are views have changed. Knowledge of the current political tension and protests in Hong Kong is useful and important here.

The text makes a point about Hong Kong's economic position, and the potential of this impact on China. It emphasises the distinction between Britain's capitalism and China's communism, while demonstrating the potential of Hong Kong to become a major economic centre. Knowledge of how this situation has changed would be insightful, and would indicate the way in which China's economic ideology has moved away from a pure form of communism to one that depends on rapid growth.

It also emphasises the experimental and transitional nature of Hong Kong becoming governed by China, which calls into question issues such as democracy and the rule of law. It could be useful to consider the extent to which true democracy could exist in Hong Kong while a British colony, and whether or not Chinese governance would in theory just be doing the same thing as Britain, albeit under the banner of communism.

Then, consider the second part of the question in more depth. Contemporary uprisings in Hong Kong suggest that views on the ground have changed, and that the extradition bills etc. have called into question issues such as democracy, independence, and rule of law. It will be useful to compare this reality with the possible outcome expressed in the article – the answer to the author's question 'Could something similar happen when it comes to politics and the rule of law?' seems clearly impossible now. You should also discuss China's increasingly autocracy under Xi Jinping, and the growing hostility of the West towards China's continued growth – useful examples would include the widespread suspicion across America and Europe that the technology company Huawei is working on behalf of Chinese intelligence services.

The conclusion will resolve the essay concisely, and give a clear statement of what we can learn about colonialism, before grounding it in broader knowledge.

Sample Paper D

How does the Bugis understanding of gender contrast with De Paiva's? And with our contemporary Western ideas? What ideas are at stake in religious conversion?

In the introduction, address the main themes that are raised by the extract and by the questions (gender, spirituality, religion, colonialism, cultural interactions etc.) and make sure you know exactly what the question is asking you to focus on. Namely, *how* all of these things contrast and overlap.

The body of the essay will hone in a few keys areas of contrast raised in the extract. From there, it will be possible to show the difference between the Bugis and De Paiva, then how we view gender today (although this itself is contentious, and will be a chance to demonstrate knowledge of current debates) and the implications for religious conversion.

The Bugis clearly believe that neither man nor woman is better, as both are removed from communication with the gods – De Paiva clearly believed in the hierarchy of men, as evidenced by his condescension of the bissus for their relationships with other men and their adoption of 'feminine' traits. The idea of 'gender fluidity' is more commonly accepted today, as many believe that gender is more about feeling and emotion rather than arbitrary characteristics. In religious terms, this is significant as Christianity and Islam both depend on clear distinctions between men and women, as demonstrated in institutions such as marriage.

De Paiva emphasises the carnal union between two men as something immoral, as opposed the Bugis' clear belief that homosexual relationships are natural and valid. Again, this is now widely accepted in the modern Western world, although some religious communities are still reticent.

De Paiva seeks clear distinction between man and woman, drawing on the Christian belief in how God created man and woman (Adam and Eve). The Bugis believe that the gods deliberately left some people undifferentiated – this opens up agency for intersex and genderfluid people, again tapping into many ideas gaining ground today.

Further points could emphasise the way in which religious conversion can lead to 'hybrid' religions; for example the Bugis operate under the banner of Islam, but continue to incorporate their fluid approach to gender.

Conclude by summarising your argument, and emphasising the ways in which differing communities have always had varying approaches to gender and sexuality.

Education

What is the significance of the 'whole language' approach to reading in terms of meeting a diversity of learners' educational needs and social backgrounds?

The keywords in this essay are 'whole language approach', learners' educational needs and social backgrounds. Defining these terms with regards to how they are used in your essay will give your essay clarity.

It is important to show that you understand what the whole language approach is referring to, and how it links with diverse educational needs/social backgrounds - does it allow educators to cater to unique educational needs or does it make it more difficult to do so? Does it bridge the achievement gap between different social classes or does it widen that gap? You can describe the whole language approach in detail and consider these points to make a strong argument.

Since the essay talks about both educational needs and social backgrounds, it is important to focus on both. You can do so in separate paragraphs or in the same paragraph as you write your essay. Think of students with learning disabilities such as dyslexia and dyspraxia or visual and hearing impairments - a whole language approach would certainly be more convenient for them. If they have difficulties reading, they can focus more on other language modes such as listening, talking and writing. Equally, children from lower socioeconomic backgrounds or those going to state schools (as opposed to independent schools) can also benefit from this approach; studies show that higher SES parents tend to use a greater frequency of words per minute when communicating with their children, which contributes to faster cognitive development. As a result, if all language domains are considered fluid and interchangeable, children from lower SES backgrounds could 'compensate' for their backgrounds via a whole language approach.

Are there any conditions under which the whole language approach would fail to meet learners' educational needs and diverse backgrounds? Perhaps if such an approach is implemented in the classroom, it may take away attention from reading as a special mode of language. As a result, children who struggle with reading might not receive additional support that they currently do - remedial classes, after-school reading programmes - and thus this may widen the educational gap for children with greater educational needs.

Now, it is time to consider the significance of a whole language approach for meeting learners' educational needs/social backgrounds. Your conclusion should answer the question based on the points you have discussed above - explain if and why the approach is significant/insignificant.

How does the 'whole language' approach to reading engage with issues around motivation and its role in learning?

The keywords in this essay are 'whole language approach', motivation, and 'its role in learning'. Defining these terms with regards to how they are used in your essay will give your essay clarity.

Try to describe the whole language approach in detail and explain how you think it can influence motivation for learning. Can it increase motivation or decrease it? What are some primary issues around motivation's role in learning that can be solved with the whole language approach? You can focus on two or three issues for this essay; I will focus on i) personal interest in the subject and motivation for learning, ii) personal capabilities and competencies, iii) lack of focus.

Spillover effects: Think of how personal interest in subjects can boost motivation for learning. If we implement a whole language approach, students have a greater chance of liking at least one topic being taught - e.g reading or writing - and thus, can perform well in it (if not across the board). This can help motivate them to keep working hard and lead to compensation or spillover effects, eventually boosting their performance even in the subject they do not have a natural preference for. Equally, if a student's personal capabilities in reading are greater than they are in writing, a whole language approach will help them cultivate greater competency in the weaker subject. This is in contrast to approaching them as separate disciplines, in which case the student may not feel as if they are capable of being a good writer, and thus will have no motivation to work on their writing.

Here you can bring up some alternate perspectives about motivation and learning; perhaps a whole language approach, due to its holistic nature, takes away the focus from individual components. If students were taught to approach reading, writing, listening as separate disciplines, they may have more time and ability to focus on each individually in the classroom. For example, if a student is already a quick reader but a poor writer, it may be a waste of time if they focus a lot on reading and not too much on writing.

Now, it is time to consider your overall conclusion about whether the whole language approach is useful for solving motivational issues in learning or not. Make sure your argument is balanced and relevant to what you discussed above.

Using some examples to illustrate your argument, in what ways might a 'whole language' approach be supported by different kinds of texts, both literary as well as non-literary?

The keywords in this essay are 'whole language approach' and 'supported by different kinds of texts'.

Give an example of the different texts in general which can be used to support language learning in the classroom. Maybe the current teaching system does not allow us to use all such texts to the maximum capacity, and a whole language approach would solve this problem. It might be worth choosing one literary and one non-literary text for the rest of the essay. I will choose Oliver Twist by Charles Dickens (literary) as well as The Daily Magazine (non-literary).

For the non-literary text, I will argue that using the whole language approach in combination with the text can be useful for several purposes. For writing, it exposes students to a more casual writing tone and style which is useful for daily communications. It also teaches them to read at a quicker pace due to the easy vocabulary used.

The literary text will enable students to expand their vocabulary, read unfamiliar texts with confidence and also use new writing styles in their work. In this way, it can be useful for formal essay or letter writing, and equally, will help them improve their listening skills in a formal context.

Now, it is time to consider the significance of a whole language approach for introducing different texts in the classroom - does the approach add much or is it redundant? Make sure your conclusion is relevant to your main body paragraphs.

Sample Paper A

Why might Engelmann's technique be considered controversial?

Highlight your knowledge of what 'Engelmann' s technique' is by defining it here. Give a starter sentence of how this might be controversial (opposition from educators or students?) and in contrast to which alternatives is it controversial.

Carve out your argument here - are there ways in which Engelmann's technique of direct instruction can have benefits? Despite its advantages, why would it then be controversial? Focus on two to three points: passive learning and lack of personalised learning. In this essay, I will argue that it conflicts with the real purpose of learning: to grow as individuals.

Direct instruction may be considered controversial because of how it may inadvertently lead to passive learning. Students sitting in a classroom, all pronouncing multiple phonemes of a word at once whilst they are instructed by the teacher to do so can be repetitive and perhaps even counterproductive for increasing rates of learning. This is because it can be very passive to follow it in a classroom, and a more student-led teaching method may be more useful for increasing student motivation and interest.

Engelmann's technique, due to its rigidity, might not be the best for catering to personalised learning needs. For example, some students are kinesthetic learners while others are visual learners. In an ideal classroom, there should be sufficient resources and support available to make full use of these diverse learning needs to enhance one's learning. A direct instruction method would, however, most likely benefit auditory learners. Moreover, it may fail to fit in well with the true purpose of an education. This is because of its rigid structure, it fails to inspire individual ways of solving problems and learning new information (e.g some might learn better with a whole word technique whilst others excel with phonemic techniques). There should firstly be room for manouevering this within an educational system, which Engelmann's structured technique does not provide.

Upon considering the issues it causes for student participation and personalised learning needs, it is easy to see why Engelmann's technique is controversial. However, it should be noted that direct instruction - in one form or another - is implemented in every classroom to some degree. It may then not be a question of whether Engelmann's technique is controversial, but rather to what extent can it be adequately applied in a classroom.

Why might teachers be resistant to the direct instruction method?

Define direct instruction, and how it is applied by teachers in real life in the classroom. Be clear with your definitions as the question uses a keyword and it is important to show you have sound understanding of the concept.

Why might teachers possibly be resistant to the direct instruction method? Focus on two to three points in the essay. I will focus on: how direct instruction does not promote curiosity and individual learning, as well as the lack of student-led learning in direct instruction.

Teachers might now be moving away from Engelmann's traditional method of direct instruction because of how it doesn't encourage students to find answers to problems themselves. Instead of promoting curiousity to find the correct answer to a problem, it involves the teacher explicitly teaching a classroom what the answer is. It thus seems to miss out on an essential step of learning: the personal discovery of reaching a solution. In a classroom of 30, every child will have his own creative ways to solve a problem (or in this case, to read), and educators now want to be mindful of this.

Direct instruction is predominantly teacher-led and inspires images of bored students sitting in a lecture theatre, waiting for a lecture to be finished. This is in contrast to more student-led teaching methods which involve working in groups, discussing ideas together and using assessment methods such as presentations. Instead of spoonfeeding the answer to students, teachers are now aware of how important it is for them to be equally involved in the teaching process. This also helps develop skills for further independent study which is crucial at university.

Issues related to student participation and lack of personal involvement in discovering solutions to problems explain why teachers are reluctant to use direct instruction in their teaching. However, this is not to say that direct instruction is all bad - it is quite useful in contexts where students are being introduced to new and difficult concepts. Perhaps it should then be more about 'when' to carefully apply direct instruction teaching methods, than to fully shun them.

Sample Paper B

If you could never tell anyone you attended Cambridge, or put it on your CV, would you still have applied?

Decide if you want to say yes or no, and briefly write down which points you will be discussing to support either point. I will argue that yes, I would still have applied, and in order to show why, I will discuss i) the intrinsic value of education, and ii) the benefits of people not knowing that you attended an elite institution.

The intrinsic value of a Cambridge education would not be erased by other people not knowing that you went to Cambridge; indeed, even as a Cambridge graduate you will certainly be in situations where other people won't know of this fact about you. Other's perceptions and judgments (positive as they may be) about you and your education are not nearly as important as what a Cambridge degree actually teaches you: to be curious, to question everything and always want to know why. It also teaches you humility, intellectual freedom, how to solve some of the most pressing problems in the world and that is just as valuable as it would be without everyone knowing you went to Cambridge.

There might even be benefits of such a system where it isn't common knowledge that someone went to an elite university - for example, stereotype bias would be erased and negative (and flawed) perceptions that people might hold about Cambridge being elitist and classist would no longer be associated with you. As stated in the passage, it can lead to equality and greater social mobility in society as people from non-Russell Group universities will have the same access to jobs and social resources as those from Cambridge.

It can be argued that there are negatives to this approach, as you may no longer gain any added benefits of going to a top university like Cambridge. For example, getting a job or scholarships for further study may no longer be as easy as they would have been if people had known. It might also motivate people less to even apply and aim for good grades to study at such universities as there may not be any extrinsic factor or 'end goal' as you can no longer make use of the 'signalling' procedure.

Although there are advantages and disadvantages to people not knowing/not being able to put this on your CV, perhaps we can conclude that this is an ideal a society should strive towards. For if there is pure equality in society, everyone - regardless of which university they went to based on what prior opportunities they had - will be able to have equal access to resources (social, economic, etc) and there would be no need to use signals such as having gone to Cambridge to guarantee better future prospects for yourself.

Defend the conventional model of college education from Caplan's attack.

Define the conventional model of college education in the UK: usually 3 years, lectures with independent assignments and group work to be handed in, tested with exams at the end of the year. Show that you are aware of how it conflicts with Caplan's view of educational signalling, and define that concept a bit more here.

You may want to summarize your argument here; what main reasons will you use to defend the conventional model of college education from Caplan's attack? You can briefly sum it up by saying: i) the benefits of a college education extend beyond the financial, ii) skills learned through college, iii)

Signalling doesn't count for half of the financial reward of college: by making this statement, Caplan is ignoring all the other benefits of a college education besides the financial. Caplan's point only makes sense if the only purpose of education is to earn money. But as different people have different values, for some things such as learning more about the world and developing holistic skills is more important. Other things such as the whole college experience and meeting so many different people, being exposed to unique perspectives through study abroad/field trips all add to the usefulness of a college education, and make students grow as individuals.

Pay rises by senior year could also have an alternate explanation; perhaps skills one learns through college aren't polished since then? Teamwork learnt through group work, the ability to work independently through assignments, communication skills learnt by discussing concepts in supervisions and seminars - all aren't perfected in one year, or even two. Course difficulty also increases with each year, so it makes sense why seniors will earn more than juniors as it shows they can have a stronger grasp of difficult concepts.

Caplan's argument is valid only insofar as we consider the only benefit of education to get a high-paying job; but for some there is more to be gained from an education - all of which isn't exactly quantifiable and goes against Caplan's argument. Skills gained through college also take time to develop, and Caplan assumes that educational signalling is the only reason behind differences in first, second and third years in college - but fails to consider alternate explanations.

Sample Paper C

How important do you see education in combating inequality?

Before discussing whether you think education is important in combatting inequality or not, define the keywords. First define inequality; do you mean class-based inequality, racial inequality or physical inequality (e.g disabilities)? I will focus on class-based inequality. Then define 'education' - what type of education? University, secondary or primary?

State an argument - you should clearly say whether education is important in combating inequality or not, and why. I will argue that it is one of the most important social factors, but only when it is implemented with societal factors which support social mobility. This will be shown through three points focusing on a) corruption and b) inequality driven gaps in education.

Firstly, adequate social structures must be in place so that education can successfully fight inequality. The primary way of doing so would be that a higher education level correlates directly with a higher job rank/pay level. This means that there must be fairness and justice within the employment system of a country - if a PhD holder cannot be appointed onto a high-paying position just because he comes from a low socioeconomic background, his education is of no use. In several societies with rampant corruption across the world, individuals with lower qualifications than required are given roles unfairly. In such societies, it is very difficult for education to combat inequality successfully. This doesn't mean there is an issue with the education system, but more so with the social structures in place.

If there are quality differences in education driven purely by social class inequality, it is very difficult for education to successfully combat inequality. For example, in the UK, a large majority of students going to Oxford and Cambridge come from independent schools and privileged backgrounds. This means that instead of combating inequality, educational systems can also perpetuate and exacerbate conditions of inequality. This can be due to low quality of teaching in some state schools, overcrowding of students and understaffing, as well as lower access to top resources (such as tips on how to get into elite universities from alumni).

So, how important is education in combating social inequality? It seems like the answer depends purely on how fair society itself is, and what structures are in place to prevent corruption and unfair employment procedures. Only if the society itself is fair can social mobility successfully be put into practice.

Do you think private tuition for university applications is fair? If not, how might universities go about ensuring it doesn't unfairly advantage applicants?

Define keywords: private tuition and university applications. Be specific about whether you mean interview help, personal statement help or both, as well as 'universities' - it might be worth saying which universities (Oxbridge or all Russell Group) you are focusing on.

State an argument - you should clearly say whether you think private tuition for university applications is fair or not. I will argue that it is not, because of access issues and class-based gaps which it further widens. The second part of this question is how can universities ensure it doesn't unfairly advantage applicants - I will answer this by giving two options: a) giving education is important in combating inequality or not, and why. I will argue that it is one of the most important social factors, but only when it is in combination with societal factors which supports social mobility. This will be shown through three points focusing on a) corruption and b) inequality driven gaps in education.

Firstly, adequate social structures must be in place so that education can successfully fight inequality. The primary way of doing so would be that a higher education level correlates directly with a higher job rank/pay level. This means that there must be fairness and justice within the employment system of a country - if a PhD holder cannot be appointed onto a high-paying position just because he comes from a low socioeconomic background, his education is of no use. In several societies with rampant corruption across the world, individuals with lower qualifications than required are given roles unfairly. In such societies, it is very difficult for education to combat inequality successfully. This doesn't mean there is an issue with the education system, but more so with the social structures in place.

If there are quality differences in education driven purely by social class inequality, it is very difficult for education to successfully combat inequality. For example, in the UK, a large majority of students going to Oxford and Cambridge come from independent schools and privileged backgrounds. This means that instead of combating inequality, educational systems can also perpetuate and exacerbate conditions of inequality. This can be due to low quality of teaching in some state schools, overcrowding of students and understaffing, as well as lower access to top resources (such as tips on how to get into elite universities from alumni).

So, how important is education in combating social inequality? It seems like the answer depends purely on how fair society itself is, and what structures are in place to prevent corruption and unfair employment procedures. Only if the society itself is fair can social mobility successfully be put into practice.

Sample Paper D

How do you understand the relationship between the state and schooling?

Define the terms the state and schooling, and what your understanding of these terms is. What is the association between the two and are they both important for each other?

You can set up an argument that the state and schooling share an essential relationship in terms of funding. State support is required to provide for school-based resources, hire teachers and build schools across a country. But perhaps this is the extent of their relationship, and anything beyond this may cause more harm than good. Explicity write that you will discuss the financial aspect of their relationship, as well as the academic aspect.

Financial; the majority of schools in the UK could not be run without state support. Taxes collected by the state directly contribute to the provision of quality education for each child across the country, and although it can be argued that the taxpayer funds this system, the state does facilitate and collect money for it to run. The government's support is also essential for non-academic activities, such as sports and arts classes available at a school. Whether the cost of children's uniforms and travel bursaries can be met also depends on the state. Overall, the state is very important for ensuring schools run adequately.

However, let's consider what happens when the state interferes too much into educational affairs beyond financials. Perhaps you can use historical examples, such as when totalitarian rulers such as Hitler and Stalin came into power, the first thing they did was influence the school curriculum. Pictures of the rulers were present in every school's main hall, and students were taught from a young age to pay their due respect to the rulers.

Another example can be when Napoleon came into power and influenced the French lyceums curriculum in a negative way. He imposed his own sexist views about what women should be allowed to do (sewing and crafting as opposed to reading medicine and law) into the school syllabus. This affected generations to come, and could have easily been avoided if educational matters were left to the academics.

Conclusion: recognize that it is difficult to prevent the state from influencing academic matters if the state is funding the educational institution. However, it is also the ideal option; if the government in power holds problematic views about a particular group in society, it can adversely affect social mobility.

Should education be centred on freedom as a goal, or focus on specific educational and social outcomes?

Define freedom as a goal and what specific educational/social outcomes can look like (e.g an A* grade or a high paying job?).

Are there any advantages to either approach - if education was centred on freedom, what would it offer individuals or society? What about specific educational outcomes? Think of what your argument will be - I will go ahead and say that education should focus more on specific outcomes due to its role as a social mobility driver.

Although educating oneself to achieve 'freedom' sounds ideal, it might be too good to be true. Firstly, it might be that achieving 'freedom' per se from conventional views in society can only be gained through reading subjects such as philosophy, sociology, history (as they offer new insights to thinking about current affairs and social norms). The value of such degrees in today's time of medicine, law, computer science might be under threat. Moreover, such degrees are more accessible for students from higher socio-economic backgrounds because of the uncertain employment opportunities they offer. Someone on free school meals wanting to study to uplift their family out of poverty may be more likely to study economics and become a banker than they are to study art and be uncertain about future job prospects. as long as the value of a discipline in society is based on its functionality, it is important to stick to using education for specific outcomes.

Here, you can argue with the question and challenge its assumption. It assumes that education for social or academic outcomes versus education for freedom are mutually exclusive. This doesn't have to be the case. In fact, motivating oneself to work hard and get an A* on a difficult exam can be liberating in its own right - it can help you push yourself to the limits and discover new strengths. Moreover, using education as a tool to help get a high-paying job is no less than freedom in its own right.

Perhaps the two claims are not mutually exclusive, and can co-occur. So far as society is structured around educational and employment based outcomes, education should focus on them too.

History

<u>Specimen Paper</u>

Compare and contrast the characterisations of Athenian democracy offered in these two passages.

From the two sources, you can get a good impression of what Athenian democracy looked like, and a sense of how it was a model radically different to contemporary and previous modes of governance. The sources allude to the uniqueness of the Athenian way, but by comparing and contrasting them, it becomes clear that what some believe to be the strength of Athenian democracy, others believe to be its weakness.

The first thing to take note of when comparing these sources is to look at who they were written by, and what for. The first extract is an anonymous pamphlet, implying that the author's view may have been controversial, and not something they wanted attributed to themselves. The second source, by Thucydides, almost entirely consists of a speech made at a public funeral. It is unsurprising, then, that the second extract is a much more favourable characterization of the Athenian constitution, as it is an attempt to pay respect to the dead and what they fought for, and maintain support by emphasizing the superiority of the Athenian model.

Pericles speech praises the Athenians for the unique nature of Athenian democracy, and credits it system for the strength the Athenians demonstrate in their city and battles. The common people are not ignorant, but well-informed, and it is the disinterested rather than the poor who have 'no business' in Athens. This is an opposing view to the one offered in the first passage, which believes that democracy is a worse form of government than oligarchy, as it allows men to be 'wicked' and that the common people would lose all of their rights under a democratic system.

Both extracts talk about wealth, and how wealth impacts ability to vote/have a public voice, implying the ways in which the Athenians/other places have decided who governs and votes. Pericles believes wealth should be properly used and not boasted about, and that it is the decision by the Athenians to place power in the hands of all – not only the hands of the wealthy – that is a point for boasting. Whilst the first source posits that when 'the lower classes flourish' the 'power of the democracy will be increased', it also says that 'poverty gives [the masses] a tendency towards the ignoble'. Although the first source is much more ambivalent than the second, understanding the benefits of the Athenian system for the masses, yet condemning it nonetheless, the fact that both sources discuss wealth and poverty demonstrates one way in which voting ability had been decided and highlights how the Athenian system was different.

Two very different characterisations of Athenian democracy – though they both see the system as unique, and almost experimental, the anonymous source (perhaps written by a wealthy man) sees democracy as the undoing of Athens rather than its strength.

Sample Paper A

Compare and contrast the characterisations of institution of monarchy offered in these two passages.

The question asks you to compare and contrast these two characterizations. Upon reading them, they appear to be completely opposed, with Paine critiquing the institution of monarchy and Burke upholding it. It is important not to forget that the question is asking you to *compare* the passages as well as contrast them. Key points to discuss include how/from where power is derived, relations between institutions of power and the people, and historical precedent.

Paine's 'Common Sense' talks about equality and says that greatest distinction is that of 'men into kings and subjects' but makes clear that he believes this division to be neither natural nor godly. Whilst for Paine, to exalt 'one man so greatly' isn't justifiable, and notes that places without a king [i.e. Holland] have experienced more peace, Burke thinks that the abolition of monarchy threatens stability, and indeed threatens 'morality itself'.

The two pieces not only have contrasting arguments, but also appeal to different concepts to form their arguments. Whilst Paine talks of natural and religious laws, Burke emphasizes the contract between ruler and subjects. By comparing the two pieces, you can argue that views on the institution on monarchy can differ dependent on how people believe authority and power is obtained – from nature, from God, or from a contract between a people and a ruler, in which power is transferred from a sovereign people to sovereign ruler. This could be a good point to talk about any theories of governance if you know any (such as the Divine Right of Kings) but you don't need to know any prior information to answer this question.

A final point is that both extracts deal with time/temporality in different ways, talking of 'chronology' and the passing of ages. Whilst Paine uses historical and religious examples of the negative impact of monarchical rule, Burke looks to the future, saying that the abolition of monarchy will cause chaos.

Conclude by saying that these texts can be compared on different levels. Firstly, the obvious way in which one supports and the other criticizes the institution of monarchy. Secondly, how different types of argument are employed to make their point – one looking at religious and natural law and the other contract. Lastly, they are both concerned with teleology and time, but this manifests in different ways. The pieces may be written around a similar period, as they seem to be arguing against each other.

Sample Paper B

Compare and contrast the rights and responsibilities outlined in these two passages.

These two passages, the first longer than the second, are written many years apart, in some ways sound very similar. When you look closely, however, there are some key differences between the rights outlined in them; in what they believe man's rights to be, in the extent of power they give to the law, and in their attitudes towards race and slavery

There are similarities – both talk about man's freedom, protection against harmful action, man's innocence until proven guilty, and man's private property. However even the ways in which they talk about these things is quite different. For example: Article IX of the first passage is similar to articles in the second, but it is interesting that this one article is equivalent to Articles 9 and 11 in the second, perhaps demonstrating a greater concern with peaceful arrest.

Both passages concerned with the impact of law E.g. Article IV 'borders can be determined only by the law', Article V 'the law has the right to forbid actions harmful to society', Article VI 'the law is the expression of general will' – 8/17 articles in The Rights of Man concerned with the law, and 5/12 in the Declaration. One Article about the law in the first passage that stands out as unmentioned in the second is Article XI in free communication of thoughts and opinions. This inclusion indicates that there had been an issue with free communication around the time that Lafayette and Sieyes were writing that needed to be addressed.

Articles absent in the Rights of Man that are present in the Declaration of Human Rights are those about race and slavery. Article two talks about distinctions not being made on 'race, colour...', something which was normalized in the eighteenth century. Article four also talks about how 'no one shall be held in slavery or servitude' – this is not mentioned in the Rights of Man, perhaps as it was not a concern or an achievable goal in eighteen century.

Whilst on first look these two passages are remarkably similar [although written in different linguistic styles], and do share a lot of points, there are some notable differences that relate to the context in which they were written.

Sample Paper C

The passage below is the first article of the Treaty of Tordesillas, in which Spain and Portugal divided up the New World between them at the end of the 15ᵗʰ Century. Write a short essay on its implications and consequences.

When approaching this essay, you should first try and think about the key words involved in the question – in this case, 'implications' and 'consequences'. One thing you may think about is how these two terms are different, and how the implications of the treaty may differ from the practical consequences. The question provides you with some information, telling you that it is a treaty between Portugal and Spain. Take into account who is likely to have created such a source, how representative it is of the views of the 'constituents' mentioned, and also the absence of those living in the 'New World' in this source.

It is crucial that any points made in the essay are based on direct interpretations of the source. Make sure to quote or allude to the section of the material that has lead you to your arguments, and explain why it has done so.

The body of your essay should not simply repeat the source, but interpret it. Some of the implications of the treaty are clearly laid out in the treaty itself. It is clearly an attempt to create a more consistent way of dividing up new territories to get rid of the 'controversy' the exists between 'the said lords, [and] their constituents'. The treaty implies that this new system will settle these matters, and that both parties are happy with the arrangement. That these lands will be divided between these two parties and 'pertain forever' to them is a key area for analysis. Would lands discovered by Portugal on Spain's 'side' of the division be readily handed over? Would the lords and constituents necessarily agree on or follow these rulings? Would this treaty be problematic for countries who later joined in with the colonization of the New World? The language of this source shows that the authors believe the New World to be a truly new discovery, which was theirs to divide up and 'possess' as they pleased, ignoring existing divisions and cutting a 'straight line'.

Make sure the conclusion is line with the body of the essay, stating clearly the implications and consequences of this treaty are, and not getting lost/start rambling. Explain how these may vary depend on whose perspective the treaty is seen from, and that what the treaty indicates is happening, and what is actually happening may be two very different things.

Sample Paper D

The passages below, from John F Kennedy's address to American University, widely known as The Peace Speech, and Malenkov's "Peace Offensive" speech. Write a short essay contrasting the two speeches, and exploring their implications and consequences.

Both authors are offering what they think are the models for peaceful existence, but their ideas as to how to achieve peace are very different. The sources demonstrate the differing priorities of the countries and the speakers, and demonstrate how Kennedy and Malenkov give different meanings to peace and believe they are in different places in the process of achieving it.

We know that the sources are from America and Russia during the mid-twentieth century, two nations which functioned very differently. Because both sources are speeches, they can be seen as having an inherently political agenda. The different political systems of the America and the Soviet Union are demonstrated through the content and emphasis of the speeches, such as Malenkov's speech claiming that the USSR has achieved a level of economic prosperity (following a 'Leninist path') and peace which is unobtainable for the 'capitalist countries'.

The emphasis of these sources is also different in terms of agency and voice. Whilst Kennedy's emphasis is on the individual (problems which 'can be solved by man'), and how many individual actions create collective change, Malenkov's speech talks about the party – 'all the people' as a collective unit.

For Kennedy, peace is something which has not yet been achieved, and he aims for a 'dynamic' peace forged through institutions which facilitate communities of 'mutual tolerance'. Kennedy wants to 'persevere' so that peace can one day be achieved, whereas in Malenkov's speech he believes that the Soviet Union had already achieved a state of peace. Perhaps Kennedy's speech is a response to Malenkov's, intentionally questioning his arguments about the USSR's stability.

Though both speeches are written about how to best obtain peace and stability, and are written less than a decade apart, they are very different in content, direction and tone. Malenkov believes peace has been achieved to an unrivalled extent in the USSR through the party and the economic stability it has brought, whereas Kennedy wants to encourage a state of peace through individual tolerance and the building up of institutions.

Human, Social, and Political Sciences

Is American politics democratic?

In your introductory passage it is essential that you define what you mean by 'American politics' and 'democracy'. Do not just assume that these are commonsensical terms that everyone agrees on. A sophisticated answer will be aware that the answer to the question might vary depending on how the terms are defined. For example, 'American politics' might refer the local, state level or the national level; and 'democracy' might refer to direct or representative democracy. You should thus consider different definitions and conceptions of 'democracy'. It might also be useful to contrast democracy with its opposite – what would a *non* democratic state look like?

A strong answer will answer the question one way or the other while also considering the rival position. In your introduction you should directly tell your reader how you intend to answer the question. For example, "in this essay I'm going to argue that American politics is *not* democratic", or "in this essay I'm going to argue that American politics is only democratic to a certain extent."

The body of the paper will then be dedicated to explaining reasons, and providing evidence, for your position. Aim to dedicate one paragraph per reason. You need to discuss aspects of American politics that threaten, or uphold, the idea of democracy. This question is focused specifically on the politics of America, so it's a good idea to only attempt to answer this question if you know quite a bit about American politics.

For example for the first paragraph you might discuss the electoral college. What is the electoral college? How does it conflict with the popular vote? And is this a threat to democracy, or does it in fact support it?

For the second paragraph, you might discuss the impact of the Citizens United (2010) supreme court case where it was decided that the government cannot restrict the amount of money that corporations spend on political communications. Does this decision threaten democracy because it gives corporations too much power? Or does it uphold democracy by protecting and bolstering first amendment rights, which are a core part of the US constitution?

For the third paragraph, you could discuss US voting laws. Some states do not let felons vote, even after they have been released from prison. Is this a threat to democracy, or a sensible restriction of the vote? Recently some states have enacted voter ID laws. Does this reduce electoral fraud, thus protecting democracy? Or is this just an underhanded way to restrict minorities from exercising their right to vote?

Finish your essay with a conclusion that answers the question and ties all of the reasons together. Your conclusion should not introduce any new points or material, and should just be a restatement of what you said in the body of your essay.

Should women have their own representatives?

In your introduction you should clarify what you mean by women having their own representatives. Is "representative" to be understood in a political sense? And in what way are women being represented? For example, you might think that women should only be politically represented by other women. Or you might think that women can be represented by men, but there should be a distinct cabinet office for women's' interests. Or you might think that women need their own political party.

A strong answer will consider both why, and why not, women should have their own representatives – why would it be a good idea? And why would it be a bad idea?

The first paragraph might address the concept of women having their own representatives who are also women. On the plus side, this would increase the political representation of women and would ensure that women's concerns are voiced. For example, a woman representative might have a very different, and valuable, insight into a domestic violence bill, or abortion legislation. You might use your knowledge from history to explain why representation for women is so important: the suffragettes, for example, struggled for many years to achieve their goals. On the other hand, you might argue that there is no guarantee that a woman will be a better representative for women than a man: there is no reason to think that women representatives will automatically align their interests with other women.

The second paragraph could discuss the idea of a government position dedicated to representing women's interests. This position could be held by anyone, male or female. This has the virtue of promoting female interests and voices without restricting the position to women only. But, on the other hand, wouldn't fairness demand the creation of a similar position for every minority group? Would this be a welcome outcome, or an administrative nightmare? And is it wrong to assume that women are so similar that they have distinctively 'female interests'? Does this protect and promote genuine concerns of women, or is it patronizing and essentializing? A strong essay will fully anticipate and address these questions.

Note that this is a *normative* question – it's about what *should* be the case rather than what is, in fact, the case. This means you are allowed the freedom to creatively imagine what women having their own representatives might be like, and how the system would work. Your third paragraph could be dedicated to your idea of what women's own representation might look like.

Your conclusion should be aimed at answering the question and summarizing the reasons you have given in the body of the essay. A strong essay will have charitably considered both sides of the issue while coming to a decisive decision about whether women should have their own representation.

Are there conditions under which the outcomes of a democratic election should be ignored?

In your introduction you should clearly define your terms. This question has many parts which should be considered. Firstly, you will need to explain what a 'democratic election' is – does this refer to a general election or a referendum? Secondly, you will need to explain what the 'outcomes' of a democratic election are. Is this the result of the vote, or the implementation of the vote itself? Thirdly, you will need to give the reader some indication of what 'ignoring' an outcome is – is this refusing to acknowledge the results of the vote, or refusing to implement it? Defining these terms will give your essay clarity.

Illustrate this with examples. A strong essay will give an example of what ignoring a democratic election would look like, versus respecting the outcome.

The body of your essay should be dedicated to the conditions under which the outcome of a democratic election should be ignored. Given your definition of democracy, can you think of any conditions which might undermine democracy itself? The body should consist of two to three paragraphs, each concerning a different 'condition' under which it might be justifiable to ignore the outcome of a democratic election. For example: if the voters were heavily deceived and misinformed, and voted for one thing meaning another would that be enough to justify ignoring the election? If the voters were bribed or threatened into voting would this even still be considered a 'democratic' election? What if the voters overwhelmingly, but democratically, voted to institute a highly unethical law (like killing all red headed children)? What if voters voted to get rid of democratic elections themselves?

Alternatively, you might argue that given the definition of 'democracy', and given how valuable democracy, it is never justifiable to ignore the outcomes of a democratic election. You would discuss possible conditions under which it might be justifiable to ignore the outcome of a democratic election, but dismiss them- with good reasons.

Your conclusion should answer the question – explain which conditions, if any, are enough to justify ignoring the outcome of a democratic election.

If you could interview a relative who lived through World War 2, what would you expect to learn about the main ways society has changed since the war, and what might make their perspective distinct?

This essay has two parts which *must* be answered, and requires a good grasp of the history of world war 2. In your introduction you should tell the reader which relative you would interview and why.

You must take time to consider what might count as the 'main' ways society has changed since the war – does this refer to technological advances? Social advances? Political advances? Scientific advances?

The body of your essay should have at least three paragraphs, each dedicated to a different way in which society might have changed since the war. An incisive essay would have a clear grasp of the distinction between the state of the world at the time of world war 2 and the state of the world now.

The question also asks you to consider what might make your relative's perspective distinct, and this will need some reflection on your part. Was your relative a serviceman who fought? If your relative is a woman, what unique insights might she have? Consider things like your relative's profession, age, race, class, etc., and how these might provide a distinct perspective about the war. A good essay will have a deep, thoughtful grasp of the state of the world during World War 2 and how one's perspective of the changes might vary depending on who one is.

Does the recent migration crisis in Europe challenge or reinforce racism?

This essay will require a good grasp of current affairs – you will need to adequately understand the migration crisis in Europe in order to write a strong essay. For these kinds of exams it is useful to read broadsheet newspapers and to keep up with current affairs.

Your introduction will explain the migration crisis in Europe to the reader – when did it start, why did it happen, where are the refugees coming from, why is it a 'crisis'?

The body of your essay should be dedicated to answering the question whether the migration crisis is challenging or reinforcing racism. Your essay should consider both sides of the issue before coming to a decisive conclusion. Be sure to clearly define the term 'racism'.

Does the migration crisis reinforce racism? You could discuss the response of the right wing press, the use of anti-refugee rhetoric, and the rise in racism-motivated attacks. On the other hand, you could argue that the migration crisis is challenging racism because of the outraged response to drowned migrants, as well as the efforts to welcome and integrate refugees. Always back up your arguments with reasons and evidence.

What embarrasses people and what does embarrassment reveal about how they regard themselves?

In the introduction you must define what you mean by 'embarrassment' – is it a feeling? What is its purpose? A good answer will analyse and go into detail – a poor answer will just assume that everyone knows what embarrassment is.

In the body of your essay you should provide examples of what embarrasses people. You could note that people get embarrassed when they are caught lying, when they have to speak in public, etc. People also get embarrassed when they are praised, and even when they are by themselves (like if I trip and no one is around to see it.) Try to provide a variety of examples that all reveal something insightful about the emotion of embarrassment.

The bulk of your essay should discuss what embarrassment reveals about how people regard themselves. Be sure to link your answer to the examples you gave previously. For example, you might argue that embarrassment reveals that we have a particular image of ourselves which can be threatened, or that we are inherently social creatures who always think that others are watching and judging us. Your answer on this point should be in depth and thoughtful.

Must all revolutions necessarily fail?

Note that this essay is asking you to answer a very specific question – it isn't asking you to list examples of failed or successful revolutions. Rather, this question wants you to focus on whether revolutions must *necessarily* fail. Make sure that you actually answer the question that has been presented.

In your introduction you must define 'revolution'. Do you mean a political revolution? What is that? Is a social revolution, like the civil rights movement, different from the French revolution? In what way? What about scientific revolutions? Make sure at every point to make it clear to your reader how you are using this term.

It is tempting to just immediately answer 'no – it is not necessary that all revolutions must fail because some have been successful.' However, this is a weak answer because it assumes without explanation that some revolutions are failures and some are successes. You must discuss the conditions under which a revolution might be considered a 'success' or a 'failure' and then answer the question in light of these conditions. What does it mean for a revolution to fail?

It is also worth considering why one might think that revolutions always necessarily fail – what theory or idea is underpinning this idea? For example, if you think that ordinary people are incapable of effecting change then revolutions will always fail if they are initiated by ordinary people. A strong essay will interrogate the reasons why you might think revolutions must necessarily fail and analyse the strength of this premise.

What are the major causes and consequences of global inequality?

Note that this question is asking about *global* inequality, so be sure you don't just reference inequality in the UK or any particular country. In your introduction you must give a definition of what you mean by 'inequality' – is inequality nothing more than unfairness, or is it just an uneven distribution of resources with no normative component?

You might note that there are different kinds of inequality – there is social inequality, health inequality, education inequality, gender inequality, and economic inequality to name but a few. If you decide to discuss different kinds of inequality you must analyse the major causes of each. Another option is to discuss inequality in more general terms.

The body of your essay must discuss the causes of global inequality. This will require you to have fairly in-depth historical knowledge. Does inequality arise out of political systems? Is it natural? What, historically, has contributed to inequality (you could talk about the rise of industrialization, capitalism, and colonialism).

The remainder of your essay will discuss the consequences of inequality. What impact, if any does inequality have on the world? How does inequality affect the markets, finance, overall happiness, health, social cohesion, educational outcomes? For instance, some theorists have argued that inequality leads to lower economic growth and lower life expectancy. A strong answer will exhibit well thought out points that are backed up by evidence and knowledge.

Final Advice

Arrive well rested, well fed and well hydrated

The AHAA is an intensive test, so make sure you're ready for it. Ensure you get a good night's sleep before the exam (there is no point cramming) and don't miss breakfast. If you're taking water into the exam then make sure you've been to the toilet before so you don't have to leave during the exam. Make sure you're well rested and fed in order to be at your best!

Move on

If you're struggling, move on. Every question has equal weighting and there is no negative marking. In the time it takes to answer on hard question, you could gain three times the marks by answering the easier ones. Be smart to score points- especially in section 1 where some questions are far easier than others.

Make Notes on your Essay

You may get asked questions on your essay at the interview. Given that there is sometimes more than four weeks from the AHAA to the interview, it is really important to make short notes on the essay title and your main arguments after the essay. You'll thank yourself after the interview if you do this.

Afterword

Remember that the route to a high score is your approach and practice. Don't fall into the trap that *"you can't prepare for the AHAA"*– this could not be further from the truth. With knowledge of the test, some useful time-saving techniques and plenty of practice you can dramatically boost your score.

Work hard, never give up and do yourself justice.

Good luck!

Acknowledgements

We would like to express our sincerest thanks to the many people who helped make this book possible, especially the Oxford and Cambridge Tutors who shared their expertise in compiling the huge number of questions and answers. Special thanks also go to Alice Bennett, Frances Varley, Amelia Hutchinson, Bushra Zafar, and above all, Hayley Webster.

Matthew & Rohan

About UniAdmissions

UniAdmissions is the UK's number one university admissions company specialising in **supporting applications to Medical School and to Oxbridge**.

Every year, *UniAdmissions* helps thousands of applicants and schools across the UK. From free resources to these *Ultimate Guide Books* and from intensive courses to bespoke individual tuition, *UniAdmissions* boasts a team of **300 Expert Tutors** and a proven track record of producing great results.

To find out more about our support like intensive **AHAA courses** and **AHAA tuition**, check out our website **www.uniadmissions.co.uk/AHAA**

Your Free Book

Thanks for purchasing this Ultimate Guide Book. Readers like you have the power to make or break a book – hopefully you found this one useful and informative. If you have time, *UniAdmissions* would love to hear about your experiences with this book.

As thanks for your time we'll send you another ebook from our Ultimate Guide series absolutely <u>FREE</u>!

How to Redeem Your Free Ebook in 3 Easy Steps

1) Either scan the QR code or find the book you have on your Amazon purchase history or your email receipt to help find the book on Amazon.

2) On the product page at the Customer Reviews area, click on 'Write a customer review' Write your review and post it! Copy the review page or take a screen shot of the review you have left.

3) Head over to www.uniadmissions.co.uk/free-book and select your chosen free ebook! You can choose from:

- The Ultimate UKCAT Guide – 1250 Practice Questions
- The Ultimate BMAT Guide – 800 Practice Questions
- The Ultimate TSA Guide – 300 Practice Questions
- The Ultimate AHAA Guide – 400 Practice Questions
- The Ultimate LNAT Guide – 400 Practice Questions
- The Ultimate NSAA Guide – 400 Practice Questions
- The Ultimate ECAA Guide – 300 Practice Questions
- The Ultimate ENGAA Guide – 250 Practice Questions
- The Ultimate PBSAA Guide – 550 Practice Questions
- The Ultimate FPAS SJT Guide – 300 Practice Questions
- The Ultimate Oxbridge Interview Guide
- The Ultimate Medical School Interview Guide
- The Ultimate UCAS Personal Statement Guide
- The Ultimate Medical Personal Statement Guide
- The Ultimate Medical School Application Guide
- BMAT Past Paper Solutions
- TSA Past Paper Worked Solutions

Your ebook will then be emailed to you – it's as simple as that!

Alternatively, you can buy all the above titles at **www.uniadmissions.co.uk/our-books**

Printed in Great
Britain
by Amazon